Hypnosport

How you can improve your sporting performances

Les Cunningham
Wayne Ralph

CASSELL AUSTRALIA LIMITED
44 Waterloo Road North Ryde 2113
30 Curzon Street North Melbourne Victoria 3051
in association with Cassell Limited, Auckland

First published 1980
Designed by Steve Dunbar
Cover artwork by Wilson Buchanan

Set in 11/12 Baskerville
Illustrations courtesy of News Limited, John Fairfax and Sons, Wanganui
Newspapers and Les Cunningham
Set, printed and bound in Australia by Hedges & Bell, Maryborough Victoria
F. 880

National Library of Australia
Cataloguing in Publication Data

Cunningham, Les M.
  Hypnosport.
  Index
  ISBN 0-930298-09-8
1. Sports. 2. Hypnotism.
796'.01

CONTENTS

Acknowledgements

For permission to reproduce copyright material the authors and publisher wish to thank the American Association for Health, Physical Education and Recreation, pp. 135-6.

Foreword

This book will fill a need felt by many coaches and serious sportsmen.

Many of us have rattled off cliches such as 'it's all in the mind', but how many competitors are systematically programming their subconscious minds in order to sustain their motivation? How many are making full use of the great powers of imagery and visualization when striving to individual goals?

Perhaps the main reason for our failure to exploit these mental powers is that we do not realize the extent to which we can be helped to help ourselves. Until now I do not believe we have had such an illuminating and practical book on the subject as this.

Firstly the authors outline the history and the nature of hypnotic phenomena and then go on to explain *how* we can achieve the mental input necessary to improve the sportsman. The subject is clarified and our interest and enthusiasm stimulated. The writers, practical workers in the field, have produced a most readable account of the subject. I found it difficult to put the manuscript down.

Nearly 30 years ago, when a Lecturer in Human Physiology at the University of Sydney, over a period of time I was more or less confined to my study chair, sitting for long hours engrossed in writing my MSc thesis. I acquired a chronically 'bad back'. For months it resisted all efforts to relieve the almost constant pain. Because X-rays and other tests did not disclose any injury, after reading all I could on the subject I made a self-diagnosis. I came to the conclusion that the condition was due to a tightening of the muscles of the lower back due to the nervous tension at the time and constant concentration. This contraction of the muscles is known to constrict the blood vessels, cutting down the blood supply, which leads to pain and further contraction, completing a vicious circle. The problem, as I saw it, was to break this circle. This was where relaxation techniques and self-hypnosis proved very successful.

Being a competitor in modern pentathlon and a swimming coach, it was a short step for me to recognize the likely connection between relaxation techniques and hypnosis in improving athletic performance.

Many interesting results came out of it. For instance, I recall a pupil training in very cold water on the Bronte rock pool one winter saying, when I signalled to correct him, 'Don't wake me up, the water might be cold'. This incident alone made me aware of the possibilities of post-hypnotic suggestion in human endeavour.

At the same time it is evident that, as the authors take some pains to point out, great care must be taken in formulating the appropriate suggestions. I remember once that my suggestions to an Olympic butterfly swimmer about how his muscles would feel during a race were not interpreted in a helpful way. Following a very poor performance he complained that during the race he couldn't *feel* his arms or the water. He didn't feel· pain from his muscles — he didn't feel anything. There is an art in formulating the right suggestions, for the sub-conscious mind apparently interprets them literally.

My experiments in the field have been disjointed. The continuing pressures of conducting a swimming school, and undertaking research in measuring failure in physiological adaption (in conjunction with my wife Ursula), along with my frequent trips overseas, have combined to slow down my work on the 'mental' approach. However in recent years, as the authors point out, in the Soviet Union and in East Germany, and, I know, also in a number of successful Western teams, a great deal of attention has been given to techniques of relaxing athletes, and psychological preparation for competition. If we want to reach out for our personal best the time is certainly ripe for us all to apply systematically the reliable knowledge which has been gathered.

Reading this manuscript has fired my enthusiasm to apply to serious competitive swimmers in my care the many practical ideas presented in this excellent treatment of an important subject.

Forbes Carlile, MBE, MSc

Preface

The ritual of modern sport has reached such a competitive stage that it is time to re-examine the role of the individual. For too long coaches, administrators and the individual athlete have concentrated only on the physical side of sport and neglected the crucial role played by the individual psyche during a sporting contest.

Certainly, better physical condition, improved equipment, and a more rigorous approach to coaching has meant that sporting performance and record-breaking ability is reaching what were once considered insuperable heights. But matched against these superhuman performances are some strange contradictions. A professional golfer, Jack Newton, can go out in the first round of the 1979 Canadian Open, scorch around the course in 64 and break the course record by three strokes. The next day, under similar conditions, he is a ten-stroke worse player. What happened in the meantime?

In Sydney's rugby league football competition we have the case of the St. George team, which, as a strong, finely-tuned and outstandingly aggressive combination, won the 1977 competition. This team was expected to dominate the Sydney competition for years, but in 1978 that same team walked on to the field to lose their first eight matches and with them went any chance of retaining their title. In 1979, virtually the same team, with the same coach, blitzed the opposition to regain that lost title. We may well ask: 'What happened in 1978?'

In cricket there is the common phenomenon of the batsman achieving a flawless and stylish century, yet, once he reaches that magic number, he is soon dismissed when he should be good for another hundred. In the 1979 Wimbledon tennis championships we have the case of Tim Wilkinson who can rattle off eighteen precise and powerful first serves in the first set of his second-round match against Guillermo Vilas, yet lose that same set on a double fault.

We could go on and on. In every sporting code such perplexing performances are almost weekly occurrences. Anyone with even a passing interest in sport would be aware of the strange influence of psychology in sport. Unexpected failures in teams or individuals are categorized under many labels — 'losing your cool', 'complacency', 'choking', 'losing the ball' or the more ubiquitous 'losing concentration'. But it's not the labels themselves that matter, since the message behind them all spells out the impact of psychological letdown or failure at a crucial stage in a competition. And it doesn't apply only to the top performers: any man or woman who plays sport, whether it be for fun, to get fit or to develop one's abilities to the utmost, can easily recognize psychological faults in themselves and fellow competitors. The woman athlete who believes that she will not win, but who has simply talked herself into that frame of mind; or the tennis player, losing his temper over a succession of nets, whose anger eventually loses him the game. Both are common examples of the intrusion of psychological pressures into sport and they occur at any level.

Then, on the positive side, who has not witnessed a team on the boil or an individual player in the full flight of a winning streak. They seem to be incapable of doing any wrong. The ten metre putt, the fifty metre line kick, quick hands and feet. . . all seem to slot into place. Boundless confidence seems to ride hand-in-hand with the success of an individual or team, and that boundless confidence is a joy to watch.

Apathy matched against fierce ambition, anxiety matched against confidence, complacency against arousal, indifference against a powerful concentration. Here we have a range of terms representing the two sides of the athlete's psychology — it is very much like the two sides of the coin which, after tossing, spell out 'heads you win, tails you lose'. And for very obvious reasons sports administrators, coaches and athletes are taking a closer look at that very important coin in the hope that the 'heads you win' approach will become more dominant.

This new-found interest in the psychology of sport has sprung from the realization that superb physical fitness and conditioning, coaching and tactics — while they can push an athlete to the limit — are often not enough. The weak link in the chain of human performance is the individual. And this individual, and his or her psychological needs, has been sadly neglected.

Modern sport, whether B grade suburban or top-class Olympic, demands fitness, style, co-ordination and tactical play, and has truly become a ritual. A ritual of speed and fine-tuning of the human body which demands that the successful individual must have an unwavering, automatic approach to the performance at hand. The demand for speed, power and co-ordination means that the performance must simply flow. There is no time for thinking about the weather, what you had for lunch, what happened last year, what the score is, or what you will do afterwards. The reality of the competition dictates that the athlete thinks of *now and only now*. For that performance to flow naturally without any psychological hindrance, the player must achieve complete co-ordination of his or her physical, tactical and mental abilities.

The concern of this book is the mind's contribution to sport and techniques for co-ordinating this essential input. The tool we recommend goes under the name of self-hypnosis. We recognize that there are many misrepresentations and misconceptions about hypnosis, but over the past twenty years there has been a remarkable clearing of the mystery surrounding the Western public's perceptions of the subject.

Psychologists, and many lay people who have experienced hypnosis, now realize that you *do not* go to sleep during hypnosis; you *do not* lose your will to the more imposing will of the hypnotist; you *do not* become dependent on hypnosis for performance. In fact all hypnosis is self-hypnosis because hypnosis is essentially guided relaxation — and relaxation is a feeling which all men and women can attain.

Self-hypnosis is essentially a state of super-relaxation and the traditional hypnotist is simply a guide who helps the individual reach that state. In the context of sport, the super-relaxed state of hypnosis, when combined with appropriate images or suggestions, is a powerful tool in motivating and helping the individual athlete achieve his or her goals.

And you don't need to be a champion athlete to benefit from self-hypnosis; you don't even have to be a casual suburban competitor. In fact one area where self-hypnosis is most useful is in assisting the many people with a new-found interest in getting fit. Many of these people have found the simplest path to fitness is jogging and here self-hypnosis can be used to maintain the necessary motivation which will help them through the painful beginnings and keep them keen to adhere to their fitness programme, how ever rigorous it may be.

We also suspect that some people adopt such individual routines as jogging because they did not excel at sport during their school years for any number of reasons, and have lost confidence in their abilities — feeling they would make a fool of themselves if, for example, they decided to take up tennis. We are certain that many lonely joggers would be much happier in their pursuit of fitness if they took on more social forms of recreation such as tennis, badminton, table tennis, squash or the various team games. Here, once again, self-hypnosis can be used to reassure the individual that his or her apparently foolish stumblings will have long-term benefits and that achieving some level of competence in a social sport is a worthwhile and very attainable goal.

Self-hypnosis involves nothing more than relaxation and suggestion and many people, consciously and unconsciously, use these techniques in their daily lives. In the context of sport, the value of self-hypnosis resides in its ability to allow the individual to rehearse, mentally, for the performance that is expected of him so that the actual performance flows automatically and without hindrance. This mental rehearsal can provide preparation for a whole competition season and is not necessarily restricted to a single event.

Hypnosis is no magic wand. It will never transform an individual or a motley bunch of ignorant, unfit and ill-guided individuals into an internationally successful performance unit. But self-hypnosis *can* be used to fix goals and condition the individual with the necessary determination to reach them; it *can* be used to rehearse the individual and team in the style and tactics necessary to achieve their goals and, finally, self-hypnosis *can* be used to develop the correct arousal level (the so-called 'psyche-up') so essential to that final success. Self-hypnosis is a very thoughtful approach to success in a very competitive arena. It is a tool which utilizes and incorporates many of the findings of modern psychology on the relationship between brain and brawn.

Finally, and most importantly, it is a technique which allows individuals to participate in any sport and play or perform to the limits of their natural abilities without being dwarfed by the drama and tension of the competition ritual. We hope we have filled a very big gap in the modern appreciation of sport.

1
AN OVERVIEW OF THE PROGRAMME

Whether you are a world-class athlete, a keen member of the local squash club or someone who is contemplating taking up a sport in order to get fit, there is a programme that you can follow. This programme will assist you in learning new skills and in improving the execution of skills you may already have acquired; however, there are three points you should satisfy before you embark on this programme.

Point number one is to make a clear decision about which sport you wish to perform in. Your selection should be a sport in which you really enjoy participating, a sport which gives you a true sense of satisfaction.

Point number two is to ensure that you do not harm yourself physically. Have a thorough medical check-up before you start training. This should be done at the beginning of every season.

The third point is crucial: in order to develop expertise in any sport, you must programme your computer. Your computer is your subconscious mind. It is essential that you allow it to work for you. This is where we come in.

Sport is the biggest entertainment industry in the world and a source of fun, relaxation and physical health for millions of people. In 1980 we see the booming interest and public participation in sport still increasing; and still a long way from reaching its peak. A combination of ever-increasing affluence and leisure time, coupled with a growing awareness of the need to keep fit, will ensure that sporting activities become an even more dominant part of our social life.

Yet it is worth remembering that, along with the increasing public interest in sports, the group of sciences which make up the discipline of sports medicine has also boomed. We now have a vast body of knowledge which can be used by coaches, trainers and the individual athlete to improve strength, speed, endurance, cardio-respiratory function, agility, flexibility, co-ordination, balance and reaction time. The *integration* of all these qualities, in terms of movement of the body, makes possible the practice of a sporting skill.

The key word here is integration—and it is notable that amongst all those qualities which contribute to a sporting skill, no reference is made to this integrating factor. We intend to redress this imbalance. The integrating factor is, of course, the brain; your computer.

Sports psychology is a scientific discipline; a great number and variety of trained, intelligent and disciplined people spend all their working hours studying the psychological inputs into sport. It is an unfortunate fact that these psychologists have generally studied only the top performers in a given sport—but it is understandable since the top performers represent an easily-measured, distinct group of people, about whom certain generalizations can be made.

There is a lesson to be learned from the elite. If we were to generalize, we would say that those top performers reached their lofty positions through the crude workings of the evolutionary imperative. Through the evolutionary necessities of superior strength, speed, endurance, cardio-respiratory function, agility, flexibility, co-ordination, balance, reaction time and the *integration* of these qualities through their psychological attitudes to sport, they have emerged from the jungle of competition to the exalted position on top of the pile.

But modern man has passed through, evolved away from the evolutionary necessities of the jungle. And he has done this through the simple workings and extension of the power of his personal computer, the brain. This power is what modern sports psychology is about: utilizing and tapping it to produce a better *integration,* a superior performance.

It is well known that most of us fail to make full use of our capabilities; even champion athletes are only using 85-90 per cent of their full potential. Any individual is capable of apparently super-human effort in times of emergency or sudden and unusual stress. When properly motivated, humans are capable of doubling their work output, something which no other animal can do.

A dramatic example of this is contained in the story of a thirty-five-year-old woman whose car fell off a jack. Her eleven-year-old son was pinned under the car. The woman was rather frail, weighing only fifty-six kilograms (123 pounds) but, because she thought her son was going to die unless the car was moved, and there was no other help available, she lifted the 1.5 tonne car with her bare hands and held it up long enough for her son to crawl out. She cracked three vertebrae in the process, through the compression of her spine, but this is simply a clear indication of how bones and muscle will break long before the will does.

The only restrictions and limitations we have on us in this world are those which we impose upon ourselves. You have all seen examples of these self-imposed restrictions in many situations. How many times have you asked somebody to do a simple task and they respond with: 'Oh no, its impossible,' or 'No way. . . I can't do it'.

In most cases when someone has this negative attitude, they have never even tried to perform that particular task; they do not believe they can do it and that is all that it takes to produce a failure. Unless you believe in your ability to achieve a goal, then you might as well forget about it; if you don't believe in your ability to attain your goal, you will always fail.

We become what we think we are. If we think of success we become successful. If we think of failure we become failures. If, on the other hand, we think of nothing, we become nothings. Remember: the whole world can classify you as a failure but you never become one until you admit it to yourself. At that moment, and that moment only, you become a failure.

Many people have overcome severe disabilities and carried on to win when it was thought their task was absolutely impossible and they were doomed to fail. One athlete, Glenn Cunningham, the great American middle-distance runner, was badly injured in a school fire in which his brother was killed. Glenn was seven years old at the time and his legs were burnt to the bone. Amputation seemed inevitable and he was told by his doctors that even if his legs were saved he would be very lucky if he would be able to walk. He told those doctors that he would not only walk but would run faster than any other man on earth. In a classic example of goal-setting and determination, Glenn Cunningham went on to win a silver medal at the 1936 Berlin Olympics and at various times held the world 800-metre and one-mile records.

And the most recent example of a person's ability to confront an overwhelming handicap came out of the 1976 Montreal Olympics. Eighteen-year-old Vladimir Markolov, the Soviet Union's number-two gymnast, competed in the men's all-round gymnast final with injuries that the doctors at the athletics clinic described as 'appalling'.

Markolov had worked since he was seven to reach the standard of his country's Olympic squad and by 1976 it seemed certain that he would win an Olympic medal. Then, during a warm-up before the final, he crashed awkwardly on his right ankle suffering, as doctors later described, massive haemorrhaging, torn ligaments and a suspected fracture.

Rejecting doctor's advice and refusing painkillers, Markolov competed on the pommel horse and parallel bars where, even though he could not dismount in his usual spectacular fashion, he scored a creditable 8.19 points in both events. However on the rings, his favoured apparatus, he scored an amazing 9.45 points — even after being penalized for dismounting simply and landing on one foot.

There are literally hundreds of other cases where people have overcome enormous disabilities to reach the top in their chosen sport. But they have all had one thing in common: they establish a goal; they believe in their ability to reach it; and they work until they reach that goal. These are the attributes that all would-be champions must have.

Your response to such endeavours may be 'I'm not prepared to work my butt off seven days a week, fifty-two weeks a year, in order to become a champion. There are other things in my life. Besides, I don't want or need to prove anything by rushing around an oval on busted legs.'

The point is that we look at the top performers in order to learn from them. Their attitudes, motivations and will to win can influence the average person's attitudes to, and participation in, their chosen sport.

People play sport for so many intertwined reasons no single one can be offered. Although it is fashionable in our highly competitive society to exclaim 'winning is the name of the game' or the more perverse 'winning isn't everything — its the only thing', the simple dynamics of winning do not explain why a person competes in a sport.

In many ways the sporting life is a mirror of our larger life and the potential we have in it. We are delivered into this world as a squawking, slimy, absolutely incompetent baby. Our years are spent trying to become competent and during this learning process we come to terms with our own psyche and our relations with others in society. The progressive development of competence has a number of consequences which are particularly significant in the development of sporting prowess.

The first of these is that the development of a reasonable level of competence encourages people to continue exercising that competence, and they will eventually come to enjoy exercising it. People enjoy doing what they are good at, whether it be playing marbles or fishing or running around and around a cinder track. The satisfactions involved in becoming competent tend to ensure the pleasures of being competent. So the sportsperson, although perhaps not as good as he or she would wish to be, gets satisfaction from sport partly because he or she does it well enough to enjoy it.

The second influence from the individual's long years of developing competence is of even more importance in sport. This is the habit of testing oneself to find the limits of your competence. We need to know 'Am I any good at that?' or 'Can I do that?' or 'Can I do it any better?' We need to define ourselves to ourselves; we need to know whether we are 'any good or not' or 'just how good we are'. We need to define our potential and if our potential is hindered or limited by the psychological barriers we impose upon ourselves then we can never know the deep satisfaction of performing at the limits of our competence.

Suppose you are to compete against a very strong opponent. You are at a physical and mental peak. Superbly primed and ready to play hard in a competition with only one of two possible outcomes — win or lose.

If you win you can keep competing and winning until a loss circumscribes your current level of competence. But if you lose, you can still experience a deep sense of satisfaction by simply knowing that you have played and competed to the limit of your ability. You have not failed. No. You have successfully defined the limits of your competence to a fine degree. One, two, three points' difference between you and your opponent is a measure of your competence. You may decide that you are happy with this current level of competence or you may decide to develop your competence even further by a more determined physical and mental effort that will ensure that the next time you meet, *you* are the three points' better player.

Take satisfaction in competing in a sport at the limits of your physical and *mental* abilities.

Everyone knows they can easily lift their sporting performance by increasing the physical input into their sport. Frequent and increasingly harder work produces champions in any sport. There is no substitute for hard training. It is easy to programme hard work tapering-off to produce a superbly conditioned athlete by race day. But how do you programme your mental inputs into a sport in order to meet a competition date? What exercises do you do? Is there a mental equivalent of the 5-BX physical fitness programme?

This is the question of interest to us and many sports psychologists around the world. Yet, if you conducted a survey of the studies focusing on this problem, you would find that the sports psychologists in the Western world have neglected this fruitful area of research. They have too many scattered interests and view sport and sportspeople simply as a more refined version of the larger society.

To American and European psychologists, a top athlete represents the ultimate in fine body tuning. That body, performing finely co-ordinated and practised movements, with nerves firing and reacting at a fine pace, serves as a benchmark for assessing all the other individual globs in their society. These athletes also compete against one another — so the inter-actions between team members and opponents encapsulates the drama and stresses of competition in the larger society.

Thus, Western psychologists study the sheer physiology of brain moving muscles, prepare psychological and reaction profiles and are fascinated by the group dynamics of team sport as well as the social structure and status within sports. Other studies are concerned with the application of sport in therapy for mentally disturbed and handicapped people.

The Eastern European countries however, are not so

altruistic. They are more concerned with winning and the structure and dynamics of their sports psychology is focused on one problem only: preparing the athlete for competition and so developing and optimizing the condition of 'psychic readiness' which is essential for successful competition.

They approach the problem on two fronts. First there is the long-term strategy which stresses the importance of maintaining motivation during training. This involves establishing a clear goal in the athlete's mind and carefully mapping out distinct steps in the progress towards this goal.

This first stage is an important part of the overall training programme that is necessary for successful competition. Although excessive physical exertion can lead to the condition known as 'overtraining', the resulting staleness can be a simple expression of laziness. Here we are dealing with mental, not physical, lethargy and this problem can be avoided by careful psychological conditioning.

In the second stage the emphasis is on 'immediate' preparation for a contest. This stage, of course, merges with the longer-term strategy, but there are particular problems at this time. Athletes get nervous before a competition, they can't sleep, they may be worried about tactics or be so twitchy that they cannot heed their coach's instructions. The difficulty here is to calm the athletes, yet at the same time arouse their competitive instincts to the optimum level. This level would have been assessed and estimated in simulated and/or actual competition in the work-up towards that final goal. At this stage the fine edge to the psyche of the competitor is honed by careful reassurance, suggestion and visualization of the final contest.

A third and final psychological contribution to the outcome of a contest occurs during the actual staging of the competition. Certain athletes may be upset by the attitudes or gamesmanship of their opponents. Some become extremely nervous and tense-up during the contest. Others may run too fast or find they are unable to adapt their tactics to the changing nature of the contest.

Through careful planning and liaison between athlete and coach, a series of signals and gestures from the coach can be used to break up the tension and divert the athlete's psyche into a more productive direction. The coach has an important role in ensuring that the athlete is not diverted from his or her planned path by the sheer drama of the competition.

What techniques do these mechanics of the psyche use to achieve the maximum possible performance from their charges? The various methods go under such names as auto-suggestion and auto-control, ideomotor harmony, autogenic training and hypnosis, but all these techniques have a basic affinity with the last mentioned trick of the trade: hypnosis. All these tools for honing up the psyche rely, in varying degrees, on the progressive relaxation, visual imagery and suggestion, which is the very core of hypnosis.

The term 'hypnosis' tends to conjure up images of stage performances with members of the audience playing out silly roles at the behest of the hypnotist. Weird and silly fun. Yet, when used in conjunction with a serious intent and a goal to work towards, hypnosis is a very powerful tool in programming and achieving top mental performance in any sport.

There are many misconceptions about hypnosis. To be hypnotized does not mean you surrender your will to the more powerful will of the hypnotist. The power which is harnessed to achieve the hypnotic state resides in all of us. There are no special forces exerted by the hypnotist. Rather he should be seen as a guide to help each person unleash the powers locked in their psyche. We intend to provide such a guide and, like all good guides, we shall follow a certain routine. First, you must have a reason and a motivation to become hypnotized. In this instance your reason and motivation is obvious: you want to improve your sporting performance.

The second stage is for the guide to dispel any misconceptions the subject may have about hypnosis. We have already mentioned one, namely that an unnatural influence is exerted by the hypnotist. Many of the other misconceptions have their roots in this fallacy. Let us repeat: the power of hypnosis resides in every individual. There is nothing supernatural about hypnosis. It is in fact very much in tune with the natural suggestive behaviour of humans; and suggestion has been used by people throughout our history.

Hypnosis generally relies on words, so the careful selection of words is crucial. Any number of words can make one feel good, bolster one's confidence and strengthen the will.

Alternatively, words can cut, make one feel small, embarrassed or offended. There are, in addition, some people who have the capacity to talk themselves sick. The power of words, the power of hypnosis — for good or ill — is dependent on the intent, or goal, and the words used to achieve that goal. You have the goal and we have a careful selection of words to offer you, but let us stress that hypnosis does not damage one's will. It does not make a person less self-reliant or dependent on the hypnotist. The frequent experience of hypnosis by normal people under ethical and controlled conditions has produced no evidence of anything which might be construed as damage to one's will or, for that matter, any other sort of damage.

A further, very basic misconception, arises from the use of the word 'trance' to describe the hypnotic state. The term trance has become so intimately connected with hypnosis that it is impossible to avoid using it, yet it carries many erroneous implications.

Although trance-like behaviour can be frequently induced by hypnosis, that is not hypnosis nor is it essential to hypnosis. People can be hypnotized and, to all outward appearances, they are no different from their normal waking state. To be hypnotized is to be neither awake nor asleep. It is to be in a super-relaxed state which refreshes, invigorates and clears the mind — allowing the psyche to absorb, with maximum impact, the suggestions which are offered to it.

The third stage involves explaining the act of hypnosis; what occurs and why it occurs. This third stage will be outlined in the following two chapters which concern the history of hypnosis, a brief history of its application in sport and, finally, some of the theories and explanations of the hypnotic state.

In the fourth stage it is essential to reinforce the original motivation. Assuring you, the subject, that your original inclination towards hypnosis, and can help you, and is still valid. We do this by elaborating on case studies from the files of Les Cunningham. We think they make engrossing reading and, coupled with some hard facts surrounding scientific studies on the physical performance of subjects before and after hypnosis, we will assure you that you can benefit from hypnosis.

At the fifth stage we describe, in depth, the tools of hypnosis: suggestion and visualization. These tools, the very basis of hypnosis, are designed to be worked into the final chapter where we provide scripts for inducing the hypnotic state. The integration of suggestion and visual imagery into these scripts is crucial to the eventual success of hypnosport. You should be clear about the goals you are trying to achieve, you should formulate realistic suggestions and practise the visualization of the events that lead to the successful attainment of that goal.

You will be aware that it is important to follow the route outlined by us, your guides. The route we have plotted is basically an expanded formula of what actually occurs in a professional hypnotist's office. Each stage is distinct and crucial to the success of the next stage. And, just as that hypnotist would not progress the subject to the next stage unless there was some assurance that the subject had successfully completed the preceding one, so you cannot jump into hypnosport at Stage 6 and expect results. You need the grounding, the anticipation, the information and explanation of hypnosis, in the preliminary stages, to ensure that you can eventually programme your mental input into your favourite sport.

2
A BRIEF HISTORY OF HYPNOSIS IN SPORT

While hypnosis has mainly had a medical application, its use in sport is not new. For the past thirty years it has been a common, albeit discreet, practice in many countries, particularly those of the Soviet bloc.

One of the first scientific reports from the Western world on the use of hypnosis in sport came in 1943 when Professor Dorothy Yates, of San Jose State College, described her experience with college boxers in the *Journal of Applied Psychology*. In this report she argued that the use of what she called 'set' was of great value in the preparation of athletes for competition. Her description of 'set' and the manner in which she used it is, in almost every detail, like the procedures used in hypnosis. She recognized this and said that her procedures produced the 'same condition without the hypnotic trance' and described it as a 'waking trance'. In the light of current knowledge, the 'set' procedure can be considered to be just one of many forms of hypnosis.

Basically what Professor Yates did was work with twelve college boxers, all but one of whom had had no previous experience in boxing. The twelve young men were paired off by a coach so that, in his opinion, they were evenly matched. Professor Yates worked with one member of each pair and, in the subsequent matches, five of those who had been subjected to 'set' preparation won their fights decisively while the sixth match ended in what was described as 'nearly' a draw. Later in the season the whole squad, working with the Yates' set technique, won their inter-collegiate contests against much more powerful and experienced competition.

In the late 1940s and early 1950s, an American psychologist, David Tracey, worked extensively, with professional basketball, baseball and ice hockey players, gaining wide publicity with the success of his endeavours.

In the classic heavyweight boxing match of the 1950s, Ingmar Johannson was conditioned for six weeks with hypnosis before winning the world heavyweight championship from Floyd Patterson, by a knockout in the third round. Johannson had previously been considered to be a huge and hulking 'powder-puff' boxer, totally lacking a good knockout punch. Hypnosis was used in this instance to instil the 'killer' instinct that helped him win the championship in 1959.

An unusual application of hypnosis in sport was provided by New York psychiatrist, David Ellen. In 1961, Jackie Jensen, a baseball player with a superlative record in the Boston Red Sox team, was about to quit in mid-career simply because he could not endure the torture of flying. Through the successful intervention of hypnosis he was able to overcome his fear of flying and continue in his winning ways.

Following the publicity surrounding the successful use of hypnosis with Jensen, Ellen became more involved in the application of hypnosis to sporting problems. Among many notable cases, Ellen 'cured' a hip injury which afflicted the ace pitcher for the New York Giants, Sal Maglie. This 'injury' would not respond to conventional physical treatment yet, after hypnosis, the 'injury' was eliminated and the very next day Maglie pitched a shutout. In 1962 and in the later years of that decade, hypnosis, mediated by Ellen, was used by Maury Wills of the Los Angeles Dodgers, as an aid in sustaining both the emotional stress and physical pain involved in setting the phenomenal record of 104 stolen bases in a single season.

During the late 1950s and into the early 1960s, Professor Warren Johnson from the University of Maryland, studied hypnosis in relation to sporting performance and also utilized hypnosis in overcoming some specific sporting problems. We will elaborate on these studies in subsequent chapters, but it is worth recounting one case here. Professor Johnson reported this study in the October 1961 edition of the *American Journal of Clinical Hypnosis*. The subject was a very successful, professional baseball pitcher who could only produce his best performances after he had whipped himself up into a rage before and during games. Attaining this fine rage was difficult, infrequent and unpredictable. But, above all, it was an emotionally draining problem for the man. Through the intervention of hypnosis he was taught how to manipulate his aggression and play consistently well throughout the season without going through the personal agony of tortuous self-motivation.

In 1972, Professor Wilfred Mitchell, Professor of Psychology at the University of the Pacific, in California, published the results of a survey into the use of hypnosis in sport.

In his book, *The Use of Hypnosis in Athletics in American Colleges, Universities and High Schools,* Mitchell surveyed the practice of hypnosis in 1641 Canadian and U.S. high schools and universities, by distributing a questionnaire to the athletic directors in each of these institutions. From the returns, some 5 per cent of universities and 3 per cent of high schools had knowledge of the use of hypnosis by their athletes in the previous twenty years. Since this usually involved only individual athletes, the overall picture showed that the use of hypnosis in sport, in any one year, was very low. However, Mitchell considered these figures to underestimate the actual situation since some of the replies did not match the personal knowledge Mitchell had of the. use of hypnosis at those institutions — possibly as a result of a natural reticence by athletes in admitting to the use of hypnosis.

What is of great interest, is the generally favourable assessment of hypnosis. Approximately 66 per cent of the athletic directors reported 'excellent' or 'good' results; if the 'fair' results are added, especially in the light of the considerations mentioned above, we find that hypnosis was of positive value in some 80 per cent of cases. Mitchell makes the point that when the 20 per cent of 'poor' or 'harmful' results are interpreted, through the various comments made, it is clear that the results were negative simply because no changes occurred as a result of hypnosis. And even these negative results should be qualified by the fact that the people performing the hypnosis were of extremely diverse backgrounds and few had experience in the application of hypnosis in sport.

However, other comments on the sports and the specific problems upon which hypnosis was used, make illuminating reading. The range of sports involved was wide with the main emphasis being placed, as could be expected, on basketball, football and track events. The other sports included baseball, swimming, tennis, golf, wrestling, water polo, archery, gymnastics, boxing and lacrosse. The specific purpose of adopting hypnosis also spanned a broad variety of applications. These are some of the purposes quoted by Mitchell:

Swimming: 'to increase stamina'.

Boxing: 'he had an awful problem of blinking his eyes and we wanted to stop that'.

Tennis: 'to maintain grip on racquet — he was unable to keep hold of it'.

Football: 'to pep up the team for a·crucial game'.

'to stop the quarterback from stuttering in the huddle';

'to set a fire under a fine player who was lazy'.

Basketball: 'to overcome first-half jitters — to forget the crowd';

'to look for team-mates and pass more';

'jump for rebounds instead of standing flatfooted'. .

Track: 'to enjoy the agony of cross-country — to take pride in it';

'to increase self-confidence after an unexpected defeat';

'to run more relaxed';

'to correct a tendency to explode in the first quarter of the race and have nothing at the end'.

As can be seen, the application of hypnosis was used to overcome seemingly trivial problems such as stuttering or blinking at crucial points in a competition through to correcting specific faults in style and tactics, then right through to the more basic problems of increasing stamina and boosting self-confidence.

Through the remainder of the 1970s, isolated instances of the use of hypnosis occasionally surfaced. In Australia, Dr Guy Grant, a Melbourne medical hypnotherapist, played a significant role in the first-ever grand final victory of the North Melbourne football team.

In Sydney, during the 1978-9 cricket tour, Mike Brearley,

the England captain, worried by a series of batting failures, consulted Dr Arthur Jackson, another medical hypnotherapist. Brearley had scores of 6,13,17,0,1 and 0 in the first three Test matches and his confidence was on a downward spiral which Jackson corrected before the Fourth Test during which Brearley tripled his aggregate with scores of 17 and 53.

Undoubtedly, in most countries hypnosis was finding a practical application in sport. But the records are patchy, being confined mostly to newspaper reports which emphasize only the 'curious' aspect. This perspective may well be rooted in the evolutionary past where strength was *all*. This has passed on to the modern generation of sportsmen the belief that power, strength and endurance are the bases of success in any athletic endeavour. No athletes want to confess that they have tampered with their psyche in order to produce an improved sporting performance. For many of them, such tampering is a reflection of a basic weakness, is artificial and, above all, unethical.

Artificial? What could be more natural than using the basic suggestibility of the human mind to programme that computer in the direction of better performance? Hypnosis offers a natural holistic approach to sport, integrating brain and brawn.

Unethical? How does so natural a technique as hypnosis compare with some of the other approaches to improving sporting performance?

At the highest levels in our sporting world, where, as the Russians have emphasized, winning is everything, not only individual but also national prestige hinges on the success of that lonely performer out there on the centre stage. The pressures to succeed are enormous. That lonely athlete has been compelled to use anabolic steroids to increase muscle power, amphetamines to increase endurance and ephedrine to provide the momentary stimulus for a peak performance. These are just some of the illegal and unethical, and unnatural, cocktails available to the athlete who cannot stand the pressure of competition. There are also legal drugs. In championship shooting contests, for example, the competitors are allowed to bring their blood alcohol levels up to a point where the alcohol has a steadying influence on a shaky hand.

Perhaps a more natural but not necessarily ethical means of

tampering with the athletes physiology is found in the practice of blood-doping. This trick involves the removal of a pint of the athlete's blood during training. At a carefully prearranged time, usually a few weeks before the crucial event, the blood is reintroduced into the veins of the athlete.

The result is expressed simply in a higher haemoglobin content and thus a greater oxygen capacity. The effect is to allow the athlete to run faster, run harder, run longer. Endurance is increased—at least for the competition period.

But what of the negative effects? Basically these can be observed in the fact that the muscles, increasingly oxygenated, are too strong for their own good. A pulled (or stretched) muscle, very rare in endurance sports such as long distance running, is a common symptom. Another more definite symptom is the appearance of jaundice, two to four weeks after the competition, when the body's self-regulating functions start to remove and reject the excess blood.

Blood-doping is termed 'natural' but it is potentially harmful and definitely unethical. What price success?

In the case of hypnosis, there is no chance of individuals being permanently damaged provided they are physically fit and carefully counselled during the hypnotic session. A footballer may be told that he will be able to anaesthetize himself against the little bumps, bruises and knocks which are part and parcel of the game. But if he does suffer some serious injury, such as a pulled muscle or broken bone, he is told that he will become aware of the fact immediately, and come off the field. He will not continue playing like a dope-crazed fiend who shrugs off all pain in this pursuit of success—a crazy, unethical practice which can inflict permanent damage on that poor doped body.

There is nothing unusual, artificial or unethical about the use of hypnosis in sport. Marathon runners have been unconsciously hypnotizing themselves for centuries—they have blotted out the oxygen starvation and the pain by letting their mind swing to the plod-plod-plodding, hypnotic rhythm of their feet. This so-called 'running high' is, of course just another variant of hypnosis.

In a similar fashion, weight-lifters focus on the shiny steel bar supporting the weight they are about to lift—they enter a determined trance. Rather than being considered unsportsmanlike, they are congratulated on their self-control, concentration, will power and determination to succeed.

Many champions have the basic psychological makeup which allows them to reach the top in their sport. They are naturally endowed with a competition mentality; their genes and upbringing have moulded their psyches into a determined competitive machine.

Examples of a natural competition mentality are many. Playing each point as it comes for example, is one competition tactic which is commonly introduced into the athlete's psyche through hypnosis: play each point as though it is the last, play each point to win. This tactic helps nervous players avoid the unsettling tension of a close contest — they are taught to avoid thinking about the score and play each point on its merits. In October 1978, Jimmy Connors, competing in the final of the Australian Indoor Tennis Championships, was blitzing his opponent, Geoff Masters. At 6-0, 4-0, the idea that he might relax the relentless pace did not even enter his head. After blasting another winner past the hapless Masters, to win his serve and make it 5-0, Connors returned to the baseline and prepared to serve again. He did not know what the score was!

Similarly, in the 1978 Rugby League Test series between Australia and England, George Fairbairn, the English goalkicker, could be observed settling himself by taking three deep breaths before every kick. As you will soon become aware, three deep breaths has an important role in self-hypnosis. Fairbairn practised it naturally.

We have already mentioned that the Soviet Union and other Eastern European countries have a long history of interest in the athlete's psyche, and this has blossomed in recent times. The simplest demonstration comes from Bulgaria where, up to the year 1959, only 20 per cent of the publications concerned with sports psychology dealt with the psychological preparation of athletes. From 1959 to 1970, the material published on this subject rose to 40 per cent.

By the 1956 Melbourne Olympic Games the Russian team supported a contingent of eleven hypnotists, a contingent with the charter to instil confidence and the will to win into the Russian athletes.

The Russians had a long time to develop an interest in the psychological preparation of athletes. Excluded from the

Olympics from 1912 until 1952, they had a healthy and fruitful gestation period, free from the pressures of competition, to study the functions of their athletes. Beginning with the 1952 Helsinki Olympics, the Russians have been the leading medal winners in four out of seven Olympic Games. In the other three games they ran a close second.

Their recipe for success is built on early selection of potential athletes followed by careful planning of the future of those young people. An eight-year-old child singled out as a potential champion and about to enter training at one of the prestigious sports clubs has already notched up several plusses on the path to success. First, he or she has gained selection. This is a coveted prize in the Soviet Union and carries with it a higher standard of living and a better education than most people can contemplate. Secondly, the parents are pleased both for their sake and the child's. The selection of their child is a reflection of their good genes and parenting and the future of their child is rosy. In any athletic endeavour it helps to have the support an encouragement of parents and friends.

The most important advantage is the fact that the child has now been locked into a cycle of goal attainment. He or she strives to represent the club in district, then the state (or Soviet) and finally the U.S.S.R., in international competition. Submerged amongst these major goals is a whole series of carefully cultivated minor goals relating to improvements in strength, power, endurance, style and match play.

Russian coaches and trainers recognize that an athlete's motivation can only be sustained at a high level when the progress of the athlete is marked by a series of successfully completed goals. In the case of that eight-year-old potential champion there is a ten to fifteen year vista of potential sporting achievements to be faced. The successful achievement of one goal is a positive reinforcement and a strong inducement to complete the next. No matter how small it may be, each goal achieved builds confidence which is immediately applied to the challenge of a new goal. The psychology of motivation, goal orientation, goal completion and reinforcement has strong roots in Russia. It is, in essence, a natural extension of the theories on reinforcement and conditioning developed by the great Russian physiologist, Ivan Pavlov.

Pavlov was awarded the Nobel prize in 1904 for his work on

the physiology of digestion but he is best known for his systematic scientific studies on the conditioning of dogs and other animals. The simplest and best-known example of the conditioned response is that of the dog who has been trained, or conditioned, to associate the ringing of a bell with the presentation of food and who will eventually salivate in response to the sound of the bell only.

But Pavlov continued his fine-tuning of the conditioned response way beyond that of the stimulus provided by the sound of a bell. He tuned his dogs so that they would salivate in response to a metronome beating at 100 times a minute but not if it was beating at 98 or 102 beats per minute. He conditioned his dogs to respond to a specific musical note and the dogs would salivate even if the note occured in the middle of a tune. Since a dog can discriminate fifty possible shades between black and white, they could be trained to react to any one of these shades; presenting the dog with a shade that was one-fiftieth brighter or darker would not induce the salivation response.

Pavlov had a very keen interest in the problems presented by hypnosis and said, on more than one occasion: 'In investigating the conditioned reflex, the problem of hypnosis and sleep kept on obtruding into the foreground'. Many animals are susceptible to hypnosis though animal hypnosis is a subject which we will not touch upon. But the great number and diversity of experiments Pavlov performed on animals, and their implications for hypnosis, led him to regard his findings in relation to hypnosis as one of the leading achievements of his life's work.

Pavlov was largely ignored by Western psychologists. In the Soviet-bloc countries, however, a whole school of thought and research developed around Pavlov's findings and, after his death in 1936, his conditioning theory and accounts of cerebral activity maintained considerable influence over research carried out in the U.S.S.R. on the higher nervous activity of man. If one had to pinpoint the essence of the Pavlovian school, it would be found in its emphasis on the mind-body interaction and rejection of the traditional Western separation of the subjective science of psychology from the more objective science of physiology. The influence of the Pavlovian school has carried over to this modern age and Soviet-bloc sports psychologists still emphasize the importance of integrating brain and brawn in any sporting contest.

The remaining history of the use of hypnosis by Soviet-bloc countries is incomplete — disguised by a natural reticence and the very basic problems posed by translation. In addition, hypnotic techniques are utilized in a wide range of psychological exercises which go under more elaborate names than hypnosis. As an example, consider the exercises involved in autogenic training.

Autogenic training involves practice in shifting to a low-arousal or relaxed condition. Trainees practise by themselves several times a day, since each exercise only takes about one minute to perform. With such frequent daily practice, the trainee develops the ability to shift into the low-arousal condition at will. After four-eight weeks of such training, a change in the physiological reactivity of the trainee occurs so that he copes with a variety of stresses without becoming hyper-aroused. The trainee has developed the ability to moderate and manipulate his arousal level.

The concept of autogenic training originated from research on sleep and hypnosis performed by the Berlin neuropathologist, Oskar Vogt, during the period 1894-1903. Vogt observed that a few patients who had undergone a series of his hypnotic sessions had practised in their own time until they were able to put themselves, for a self-determined period, into a state which appeared to be very similar to the hypnotic state. During the induction of these auto-hypnotic states, associations of feelings of heaviness and warmth appeared to be of special functional significance. The patients reported to Vogt that these 'autohypnotic rest' exercises had a remarkable recuperative effect and could reduce the effects of fatigue and tension.

Stimulated by Vogt's observation, a Berlin psychiatrist and neurologist, J. H. Schultz, began to explore the therapeutic potential of hypnosis and various forms of suggestion. Schultz' main concern was to find a therapeutic approach which could reduce or eliminate the unfavourable aspects of contemporary hypnotherapy, such as the passivity of patients and their dependence on the hypnotist. Schultz aimed to place the onus of therapy back onto the patient. To this end, by 1956 Schultz had devised six psycho-physiological exercises which form the

Les Cunningham (centre) and Canterbury-Bankstown rugby league coach Malcolm Clift (left) watch a match against Eastern Suburbs, 1976.

Canterbury-Bankstown half-back Steve Mortimer makes a break from the scrum base. After consulting Les Cunningham before the 1978 semi-final, he produced 'the most brilliant individual effort of the season'.

basis of autogenic training as we now know it. These standard exercises are practised in a quiet environment while lying down with eyes closed:

Exercise One:	focuses on a feeling of heaviness in the limbs.
Exercise Two:	focuses on the cultivation of a sense of heaviness in the limbs.
Exercise Three:	deals with cardiac regulation.
Exercise Four:	consists of passive concentration on breathing.
Exercise Five:	cultivates a sense of warmth in the upper abdomen.
Exercise Six:	cultivates a feeling of coolness in the forehead.

The practitioner of autogenic training is instructed to be passive and not pursue the training with any intensity or compulsion — 'just allowing it to happen'. Generally a trained clinical psychologist is required until the individual has learned how to master the essential relaxation response alone.

This combination of relaxation (Exercises One, Two and Four — basic hypnotic techniques) and biofeedback exercises (Three, Five and Six) which comprise autogenic training, is considered to be of particular value in the period immediately prior to the competitive performance. Quite simply it relaxes the athletes and allows them to tune into their own body image. The cultivation of feelings of warmth and coolness gives them the idea that they are fully in charge of their bodily functions, a feeling which, hopefully, may be translated into a winning image — a very basic psyche-up on the body image which a coach hopes may lead to an actual victory.

Make no mistake about that period immediately before the competition: top athletes through to weekend players can suffer the stress of simple stage fright. A survey by Dr G. Naruse of 125 Japanese champions who had just returned from the 1960, Rome Olympics, is quite apposite.

Naruse found that nearly every one of the 125 champions experienced various manifestations of 'sometimes severely disturbing psychoreactive stress and stage fright before and during competition'. Yet only 20 per cent of the group had attempted to develop some means of dealing with these debilitating reactions, and only a few of these adopted a systematic approach to the problem.

In the majority of these cases both athletes and their coaches believed that will-power, discipline and intensive training are all-important and that this makes the use of psychological techniques or assistance irrelevant to the eventual success of the athlete. Accordingly, they made no attempt to deal with the problem of stage fright.

In a follow-up study Naruse used autogenic training, hypnosis and meditation along with other psychological exercises aimed at a 'mental rehearsal' or 'mental warming-up' prior to competition. The results were reported to be very rewarding.

In a similar approach to that involved in autogenic training, Dr Laurence Morehouse, founding director of the Human Performance Laboratory at the University of California, has developed a technique for preparing athletes for competition. This system, termed 'dynamic relaxation', provides one of the few examples of Western sports doctors showing an interest in the importance of the psychological input into sport. Dynamic relaxation is basically an extension of the relaxation system devised by an American physician, Edmund Jacobson, and it is appropriate that we first describe Jacobson's system.

Jacobson first began to study the relaxation response in 1908 at Harvard University. In 1929 he published his book titled *Progressive Relaxation* which has since gone through several editions. Quite simply, Jacobson believes that there is a direct relationship between the skeletal muscles and the emotions, control of one implying control of the other.

The technique of progressive relaxation is very straight-forward — lying in a resting position, the individual alternately contracts and relaxes a muscle with decreasing intensity until contraction is nearly imperceptible. Once nearly imperceptible levels of tension are felt, these can be modulated and reduced even further. This procedure is applied to all the large skeletal muscles, usually beginning with the feet.

Progressive relaxation has been most widely used as an aid for insomniacs trying to get to sleep, but Morehouse has developed the system so that it is used in a waking or 'dynamic' state, by changing the premise of progressive relaxation from the manipulation of relaxation to the manipulation of tension. Practitioners of dynamic relaxation are advised to relax their muscles progressively and then adjust the tension upward to what they consider to be an optimum for their individual performance needs.

Again this is a very basic psyche-up of the body image — attempting to create the feeling within athletes that they are in full control of their bodies and can manipulate their muscles in such a way that they can achieve a winning performance.

The parallels between the relaxation involved in autogenic training or dynamic relaxation and the guided relaxation of hypnosis are very real: compare the six exercises outlined for autogenic training and the basis of dynamic relaxation with the scripts we offer in our chapter on self-hypnosis. However, the basic difference between these systems and hypnosis lies in the fact that autogenic training or dynamic relaxation are more attuned to relaxation and are non-specific; their main value lies in relaxing the subject, dissipating tension and developing a positive body image in the short period before a competition. With hypnosis we are dealing with relaxation *plus* a goal orientation. We deal with specifics in hypnosis; the specific orientation may be to reduce stuttering or increase stamina, or any number of things. But its most important component is goal orientation; a goal orientation which is crucial to the success of any athletic endeavour.

There are a great number and variety of publications emanating from the Soviet-bloc countries on the psychological preparation of athletes for competiton — but often these are lost in the jargon, the language and finally, the translation.

If we were to offer a translation of the Russian language and jargon it would emphasize how the Soviet-bloc countries fine-tune their athletes. In their desire to mesh brain and brawn we find the Soviet coaches operating in a similar vein to a Western motor-mechanic finely tuning an engine. And it could be argued that the racing-car mechanic should really be an athletics coach because he is a simple victim of circumstance — born into a machine-oriented, power-worshipping society he is deprived of the pleasure of fine-tuning a physically fit athlete. But this has always been the distinction between East and West.

In the U.S.A. particularly, the basic pleasures involved in

movement and power have influenced sports psychologists so that they have a peculiar learning towards the simple neurological interaction between nerve and muscle.

The Soviets and their cohorts, always foot-oriented and deprived of the sheer hedonistic pleasures of the motor-car, have directed their interests in another direction. Instead of fine-tuning a motor, they have concentrated on the mind, the will that directs those ever-walking feet. If they fine-tune their athletes with the same devotion that a mechanic prepares a car for the 'Indianapolis 500', you cannot criticize their motives. Both the mechanic and the psychologist want their charges to win.

Criticism of the Eastern bloc countries because of the apparent extremes they went to in the preparation of their athletes reached an hysterical peak at the 1976 Montreal Olympic Games. In one very typical outburst Frank Shorter, winner of the marathon gold at the 1972 Olympics, ran second behind an East German. Asked whether he would be tempted to try for the gold at the 1980 Moscow Olympics, Shorter's cynical reply was: 'Yeah, if I can find some good doctors'.

This is not a very sportsmanlike attitude and in many ways is a sad reflection on Shorter's preparation for the contest. The doctors that Shorter and many of the other United States athletes should be cultivating are not pharmacologists or even physiologists but psychologists — mechanics of the will. As a prime example, contrast the attitudes and performances of the United States women swimmers against their East German counterparts.

Look at these statistics: at the 1972 Munich Olympics, American women swimmers dominated their events, winning six individual and two relay golds. East Germany won none.

In the 1976 competition, East German swimmers won ten individual and one relay gold. The United States team had to be content with a single relay gold. A similar picture is painted in the statistics surrounding the performance of the American and East German women in the track and field events.

One of the first things to notice about these relative performances is the serious gulf between the Americans and the East Germans in terms of their physical preparation for competition. East German women are treated as the equals of men in any training programme and are trained to the same physical limits as the men.

An East German woman swimmer spends a minimum of 25 per cent of her training time in out-of-water activities such as weight-lifting and other body-building exercises. In contrast, Shirley Babashoff, at the time considered to be America's top woman swimmer, was training for approximately five hours a day but only thirty minutes or roughly 10 per cent of her time was spent with weights. This very basic problem of building a taut body was further compounded by treating the weight-lifting sessions as a diversion from the other more 'serious' training of pounding up and down the pool.

The East German women had successfully spanned that great tableau of goals leading to the Olympics. Those goals may have involved relatively simple things like the correction of a fault in style which could improve their time over 200 metres by 0.01 of a second. But they were goals. And they were positive in their pursuit of such goals. Now that they had achieved their penultimate goal of representing their country at the Olympics, they approached their ultimate goal with deadly seriousness: they intended to win.

And the way they went about it involved heavy work, both in the pool and out of it plus a deep psychological input — reinforcing all the goals they had so successfully completed in the lead-up to the Montreal Olympics. They were deadly serious in their approach since they had spent a large part of their life working to achieve that goal.

The American swimmers were much more aware of their femininity. Hard work and weight-training, producing bulging muscles, was not compatible with their body-image of the sylph-like, free-flowing swimmer who would conquer all because the United States had traditionally won and was the best country in the world. They had good food, good coaches and all they had to do was grind up and down that pool, go to Montreal, win the gold and then, still sylph-like, go home and marry the tousled-haired boy of their dreams and live happily ever after.

To quote the *New York Times:* 'There is an unmistakable difference in the social patterns and life-styles that set the Americans and East Germans apart. American swimmers . . . are a giggly group of upper middle-class teenagers, the kind you might expect to find in one of those old Frankie Avalon beach movies.'

Olympic competition demands more than the ability to play in a B-grade movie. At the highest level of any athletic contest, sports psychologists should be carefully nurturing and developing their charge's will to win; and this demands that any ideas of masculinity or femininity are of secondary importance.

One description of the degree of mental preparation East European athletes undergo comes from an Australian rowing coach, John Welch, who accompanied the Australian rowing team to the world championships at Lucerne, Switzerland, in 1974. Welch had just retired from rowing and intended taking up coaching. He decided that before teaching others the mistakes he had learned, he should observe the world's best in action.

Welch had the opportunity to come in close contact with the top rowing teams — Russian, East German and Hungarian — and one thing which stuck in his mind was that all these crews were obviously highly mentally disciplined in their approach to the championships. Several times he came across these teams on their way to training and, to quote Welch: 'The East German team, for example, would arrive, get out of their truck, go to the shed, pick their boat up with no conversation, no mucking around, just silence and they were straight out onto the water and rowing. It was obvious that they had had a very deep psychological preparation, even for training.' In contrast there was much ribaldry and chiacking, only natural amongst fit young men, before crews from the West launched their boats.

Welch was not allowed to observe the psychological preparation of the champion crews but it was obvious that it was built around techniques of relaxation and suggestion. Subsequent experiences, when Welch umpired at the 1977 World Junior and Senior Championships, and again in 1978 when he took in all three championships — junior, senior and light-weights — confirmed Welch's original observations on the importance of mental preparation.

In a chapter on the psychology and application of hypnosis to sport, it would be remiss of us if we didn't give some details of Les Cunningham's experience of hypnosis in sport. These experiences run back to 1949 and 1950, when Cunningham first used hypnosis to correct the awkward running style of Bob Baxter, a New Zealand sprinter and footballer. Baxter used to run with his shoulders up and head down, a style which approached that of the hunchback of Notre Dame. Through the intervention of hypnosis, Baxter was taught how to relax his shoulders and run in a more conventional fashion. The effect was to reduce Baxter's time for the 100-yard sprint from 10.2 to 9.9 seconds, or a real gain of three yards in a hundred.

The success of his early experiments with hypnosis propelled Cunningham into full-time study and the eventual professional application of hypnosis to both medical and sporting problems. The range of sports involved in these applications is extremely diverse — from snooker to football — and Cunningham's interest in applying hypnosis to sport continues to this date. We present a number of his case studies later in this book.

3
A HISTORY OF HYPNOSIS

The history of hypnosis is a history of suggestion. Man has always used suggestion, usually in an unconscious fashion. Our early ancestor, the caveman, felt hungry, thought of food, and the image of a brontosaurus steak or some soft, sweet plant roots, evoked a response. First off, he salivated and then, depending on the strength of the image in his mind's eye, he went hunting or gathering. Feeling, suggestion and a response.

All of us are aware of the power of suggestion. Pointing the bone or sticking a needle in a voodoo doll have both led to the death of unfortunate individuals who believed they were doomed to die. The thought of a delicious meal makes us salivate in anticipation. We touch or hear water and feel the need to urinate.

In the supposedly more advanced and sophisticated Western societies, we find terminal cancer victims who respond to new 'wonder' anti-cancer drugs yet relapse and die as soon as they find out that the latest tests have shown the new wonder drug to be useless. This placebo effect, whereby patients often show dramatic responses and recoveries from an illness after ingesting mere sugar or chalk, touted as the prescription for their ills, is a common phenomenon in medicine.

As a powerful example of the value of the placebo or suggestion, it is worth recounting the case history of a cancer patient as quoted in the American journal *Science*. The patient in an advanced stage of the disease was included in an experimental study of the since-discredited drug Krebiozen. After one injection, his tumours disappeared. As studies on Krebiozen accumulated it was concluded that the drug was worthless; when the patient heard these reports he became bed-ridden once more and deteriorated rapidly. His physician, in a last-ditch attempt to save him, told him not to believe what he had read and treated him with 'double strength' Krebiozen, which in reality was an injection of water. Again the man experienced a rapid recovery from his disease — until the American Medical Association and the United States Food and Drug Administration, in a joint announcement, pronounced the drug to be worthless. The man died within a few days.

The development of hypnosis has followed the evolution of man's ideas and perceptions of his body and surroundings and, as would be expected, has been influenced by the knowledge of the day, and the suggestions which flow from that knowledge. We have already indicated that hypnosis is more in tune with the natural suggestive behaviour of the human mind than it is with the public demonstrations and often perverse performances of the stage hypnotist. We ask you now to scrub your mind clear of any perceptions and preconceptions about hypnosis that may be resident there, scrub it clean of what you think hypnosis will do for you. We are now going to present you with a new insight into the powers of hypnosis and its practical application in a sporting context.

What better way to start than with a history?

When we look back we find that the use of suggestion occurs repeatedly in the historical records of man, usually in the context of healing or curing disease. The ancient Egyptians created sleep temples, which were just that: priests would put sick worshippers to 'sleep' and suggest that they would be cured. A stone pillar, dated at 1000 B.C., carved with the details of a 'sleep' session, survives.

The success and popularity of the Egyptian sleep temples led to their introduction to Greece and, by the fourth century B.C., sick pilgrims flocked to Epidaurus where a temple to Asclepius, the Greek god of medicine, was located. Here the sick were put to 'sleep' by the priests and through further suggestion were encouraged to see visions of the gods and experience a cure. One hundred years later the sleep temples appeared in Rome and continued functioning during the golden period of the Roman empire.

It is questionable as to whether the spread of the Roman empire was responsible for introducing the concepts of suggestion-sleep and cure throughout Europe, or whether such ideas arose independently. After all, shamans, witch-doctors and medicine men have been around for a long time, and in all cultures.

However, the concepts and the practice of suggestion to achieve a desired response persisted and changed; evolving along with man's ideas and culture. By the time of the reign of the English king, Edward the Confessor (1042-1066AD), the idea of the 'laying on of hands' was introduced, with Edward practising and perfecting the 'Royal touch'. This ritual not only appealed to the vanity of the king but was also popular with his subjects and it soon became the custom of the king to remove the ill vapours afflicting his subjects by touching or stroking the individual with the royal hand. Soon the procedure was recognized by the church in England and a proper procedure for the ceremony was laid down: a priest had to be present and, while he quoted a passage from the Bible concerning the 'laying on of hands', the king touched the sick subject and effected the cure.

During the Middle Ages hypnosis was kept alive by sorcerers and wizards. Flourishing under the cloak of black magic, it came to be considered more of an evil than a beneficial power. The roots of the subsequent opposition to the development and use of hypnosis and many of the current misconceptions about hypnosis may be found in this period. It is unfortunate that such ancient and outmoded beliefs still linger on.

However, by the early years of the sixteenth century, the role of the imagination in the development of disease was being further explored. In this period of intellectual ferment, man's continuing fascination with the magnetic properties of the lodestone (the mineral magnetite), saw the influence of magnetism intrude into the study of hypnosis. The interest of man in his psychic sphere was about to take a big step out of the dark ages.

The famous physician, Paracelsus (1493-1541), effected his cures through the use of 'sympathetic magnetism'. Searching for the life force inherent in the 'magnetic stuff' of every human body, he believed that this 'magnetic stuff' attracted chaos from the rest of the universe, particularly the magnetic irradiations from the stars. Paracelsus was also a keen observer of other medical practices and in one of his publications he describes in detail how the monks from the Cloister, near Karnter Ossiach, healed local patients by inducing them to gaze into a crystal ball until they fell asleep. He also describes examples of idiosyncratic behaviour which is common grist to the modern professional hypnotherapist.

A contemporary of Paracelsus was Heinrich Agrippa (1486-1535), who was much more explicit in his description of the psyche: 'The fluctuating emotions, springing from fantasy, not only influence our own organism but take strong effect on others — granted the fluctuations are sufficiently powerful. Thus they can bring about the cure of others as well as induce mental and psychic sickness in them. A superior psyche, blessed with vivid imagination, can evoke health as well as sickness in his own body as in that of another.' With reference to the black magic powers of fascination and bewitchment, he wrote: 'the essence of the power of enchantment is rooted in the psyche's own strong, unwavering desire to attain these ends'.

For publicizing his work, and because he was conjuring with nature and bewitching both men and animals, Agrippa found himself in prison; only being released after he performed successful cures by means of magnetic, that is hypnotic, activity.

Both Agrippa and Paracelsus achieved great authority amongst the physicians of that day who 'conjured with nature'. These conjurors combined herbs and simple chemical salts and hypno-suggestive procedures with complex ceremonies to produce the magic formula for a successful cure. If the patient didn't get better, if their state of health worsened or they died, the physician-conjuror would attribute the magic failure to the fact that the ceremony had not been conducted exactly as prescribed: a day wrong in the anticipation of the full moon, the wrong order of addition in the preparation of the herbal medicine. . . there were many sources of error. Yet, before we develop a cynical smirk, it should be noted that there were a number of totally successful cures and there is no doubt, that the principles of hypnotic suggestion had a pivotal role in many of them.

We now come to the birth of modern hypnosis with the introduction to this world, in 1733, of Franz Anton Mesmer. His contribution, Mesmerism, is to a certain extent still perceived under the persistent shades of black magic. Mesmer is still considered to be a charlatan and there is no doubt that his personality and behaviour helped to colour his reputation.

He was not modest and his antics were, at times, outrageous. But he was at the same time intelligent, flexible, if strong willed, individual who pursued his ideas with a fervent pleasure. The fact that these ideas and writings were basically wrong, is not important — they represented a quantum jump in man's perception of his psyche. Mesmer's ideas were rooted in the concepts developed by Agrippa and Paracelsus and all who had preceded them, yet they had the quality of a great scientific leap forward.

Mesmer's interest in illness began when he was present on the occasion of a wood-cutter's leg being shattered by a falling tree. Mesmer noted that as soon as he approached the injured man, who was bleeding profusely, the flow of blood was diminished; when he withdrew a short way, the flow resumed. Moving closer, Mesmer found that all he had to do was pass his hand to and fro over the wound, and the bleeding ceased. From this point on, Mesmer became fascinated by human disorders and his personal influence on the course and final outcome of the human problem.

Originally destined to study theology and enter the church, Mesmer changed tack and went on to study medicine in Vienna, under the tutelage of a Jesuit priest who bore the unfortunate name of Father Maximilian Hell. Mesmer was already an amateur student of the cosmology of the day and a good musician, in which capacity he became a friend of Mozart.

This musical interest intruded into Mesmer's philosophy and explanation of illness. At first, Mesmer viewed illness as a simple disharmony not only within the individual but between the forces resident within that individual and the larger, enveloping cosmic forces. Here he meshed together the theories of Paracelsus, Agrippa and Father Hell with the basic theories of Sir Isaac Newton, who 'discovered' the law of gravity.

However, continuing evolution of this basic idea led to Mesmer's theory of 'animal magnetism'. Simply put, this amalgam of the ideas of the time described an invisible, universal fluid, with magnetic properties, that pervades the universe. To be ill meant that there was a faulty distribution of the universal fluid within that individual. Certain people, including Mesmer, could store this magnetic fluid and will it to leave one area and concentrate in another, thus effecting the cure.

Mesmer's great contribution to the development of hypnosis lay in the fact that, following the theories of cosmic and planetary influences upon the human body he arrived at the hypothesis that the miraculous curative powers of the universal fluid resided in human beings and was manipulable by them. Hypnosis, suggestion or animal magnetism, as it was known then, now concentrated on people instead of gods and other cosmic forces. The power of suggestion was now being studied where it really mattered — in man and influencing man.

Mesmer's ideas, combined with his natural flair and ability as a showman, meant that they were an instant popular success. With patients such as Marie Antoinette, and other members of the French nobility, this popularity snowballed. The scenes in Mesmer's clinics must have been, and were hysterical. It became the fashion to experience the kicking and screaming that was the turning point, the sign that a cure had been effected. Imagine the scene. Around a large magnetic bath, filled with iron filings and with iron rods sticking out of the sides, which the patients had to grasp while they received the magnetic flow, Mesmer would fervently outline his ideas and the principles of the cure. Many of the patients were already hysterical, a state heightened by the general pandemonium, the air of expectancy, the soft music and the magnetic influence of Mesmer himself. Whirling round the clinic in his longflowing purple robe, he would mesmerize people with a long glass wand, generating a magnetic hypnotic state. And the expectation of the cure and the hysterical relief from the symptoms (well recognized by modern psychotherapists) helped ensure success.

Because of his abilities — although it should be pointed out that he probably never cured a disease of organic origin in his life — Mesmer inevitably attracted the interest of a sceptical and jealous medical fraternity who were incensed by the antics and popularity of this medical showman. Falling foul of the medical establishment in France, the government set up a committee, in 1784, under the auspices of the French Academy of Science, to investigate Mesmer's claims.

Mesmer may have been able to satisfy the committee except that by this time the demand for his cures was so great that he could not cope with the constant stream of patients flooding into his clinic — only thirty patients at a time could be treated in the magnetic bath. Mesmer's solution to this problem was to mesmerize various objects and, in his fervent and convincing way, assure the patient that, if they fondled the mesmerized object, the effect was the same as if they had experienced a personal mesmerization. Unfortunately, at the time of the committee's visit to his clinic, Mesmer was in the process of mesmerizing trees which a crowd of milling, hysterical patients were in the throes of fondling and stroking.

The committee did note that many of Mesmer's patients appeared to be cured but they were also sharp enough to notice that several of those who were cured had fondled trees that were not mesmerized. The committee's conclusions were that Mesmer's cures were simply the result of 'imaginative fancy' (read *suggestion*) and that, henceforth, the use of Mesmerism should be banned in France.

At this stage Mesmer gave up the ghost and retired from practice, seeing out his days as a canary breeder. Many others retained an interest in Mesmerism, however. The kings of Bavaria and Denmark, along with the Czar of Russia, ordered their doctors to acquaint themselves with Mesmerism and test its therapeutic and practical consequences. In addition many private practitioners continued to explore the use of animal magnetism.

The Marquis de Puysegur discovered that a magnetic bath was not essential for successful mesmerization, and that it was not necessary to induce convulsions in patients to effect the cure. Simple hand passes over the prostrate patient were enough to send the patient into therapeutic hypnotic 'sleep' — a rediscovery of the knowledge lost with the ancient Egyptians. Post-hypnotic amnesia was discovered and a famous London surgeon, Dr John Elliotson, began preparing his patients for surgery by mesmeric-magnetic treatment.

The result of these findings was that hypnosis went through a phase of rapid evolution that led to the birth of modern hypnosis when a Scottish ophthalmic surgeon, Dr James Braid, went to see a mesmerizing show. The star of the show, Monsieur la Fontaine, had recently created a sensation by mesmerizing a lion at the London zoo.

The year was 1841 and Braid went to the show convinced that the whole thing was a swindle and determined to expose it as such. While volunteers from the audience were being mesmerized, Braid examined them; he was impressed. From those observations and through experiments with friends, Braid correctly deduced that eye fatigue was crucial in inducing the trance and that a person's susceptibility to hypnosis was increased by a heightened air of expectation.

Braid published his first book on hypnosis in 1842, and here he introduced the terms hypnosis, hypnotist and suggestion, in the sense that they are used today. On the basis of his theories on hypnotism, Braid worked out a fairly simple procedure for hypnotizing subjects: a bright, shining object such as a glass prism, glass ball or candle flame, was positioned in front of the subject, slightly above eye-level, and the subject encouraged to focus on this object, staring until, with no other influences at work, the eyes grew tired, the eyelids eventually quivering, then finally closing, while at the same time there was a fatigue of the 'inner eye of the mind'. The consequence was a simple hypnotic dynamic during which everyone of Mesmer's experiments on humans could be demonstrated, including the Mesmeric cures.

In Braid's hypnosis, the hypnotist did virtually nothing. The subject stared, tired and slid naturally into the hypnotic state. Only much later was the use of verbal suggestion 'you are growing tired, very tired. . . ' introduced into the hypnotic routine. It is well to remember this. For every person who has ever been hypnotized has hypnotized himself. Magnetic looks from the hypnotist, the soothing voice, the commands to close eyes and drift into the hypnotic state are of secondary importance since the power to hypnotize resides in every individual.

Returning to Braid, it must be pointed out that he was a surgeon above all else and recommended and applied hypnosis primarily for purposes of surgical anaesthesia. In those days the so-called art of surgery constituted little more than lopping off diseased or wounded limbs or occasionally grubbing around inside the body, with no anaesthetic, no disinfectant or antibiotics and very little chance of recovery. Indeed a leading surgeon of that time actually expressed the opinion that the manual skill involved in surgery was no more than that required by a carpenter, to which a carpenter may have fairly replied that at least they knew how to mend a table or chair whereas the surgeon was content to lop off a broken leg and consider the job finished.

The horror, the pain, the 50 per cent survival rate—and even then, if the body was still intact, it was only a broken shell of its old self—made the choice easy for most people who needed surgery: they chose to go without. For those who consented the only anaesthetic available was the stupefaction available from alcohol.

Dr James Esdaile was a personal friend of Braid and, during a long period of service in India, he experimented with Mesmeric passes then later turned to Braid's hypnotism to induce anaesthesia before surgery. He was successful but like so many other successful practitioners of hypnosis, he aroused the suspicions of the medical establishment.

A government committee was appointed to examine Esdaile's claims. In contrast to Mesmer's experience, the final report of the committee was so favourable that Esdaile was confirmed in his post at the Calcutta hospital and encouraged to continue with his investigations into hypnosis. His successes grew larger. Hypnotic anaesthesia not only eliminated the pain, it increased the number of effective operations: there was less bleeding, no post-operation shock, the wounds healed quickly and the mortality rate was reduced from around 50 per cent to the more reasonable figure of 5 per cent. Perhaps the most dramatic example of Esdaile's success, an example almost inconceivable to the modern patient totally dependent on chemical anaesthetics, was the painless removal of a huge bone tumour of the face. This tumour, which covered half the face and throat, was cut out after the patient was hypnotized; he experienced no pain or post-operative shock and experienced a normal and successful recovery.

Since an effective chemical anaesthetic had not yet been discovered and since hypnosis demonstrably increased the effectiveness of surgery, large numbers of doctors began to learn how to use it. Then, just as it seemed that hypnosis was about to be officially and generally recognized and accepted, chloroform was introduced into surgery by Sir James Simpson in 1847. Its use on Queen Victoria during childbirth in 1853, put the royal seal of approval on the new anaesthetic. And hypnosis was again relegated to the theatres and fairs.

In 1889 Sigmund Freud, then a young neurologist in Vienna, went to France to observe and study the work of several doctors who were still interested in hypnotic

Steve Mortimer of Canterbury-Bankstown wins the ball from Manly's John Gibbs. The match, and the motivational build-up, are described in Chapter 5.

Sydney University Junior Eight, 1976, after winning the Riverview Gold Cup.

phenomena. Freud was enthusiastic about hypnosis but quite suddenly he declared it to be useless and discarded it in favour of the free association technique he was then developing. Since Freud's influence permeated the whole medical establishment, this decision further retarded any interest in, or development of hypnosis.

Why he suddenly rejected hypnosis is unclear. It has been claimed that Freud, a quiet introverted character, was not a good hypnotist, while others, indulging in a little Freudian analysis, have suggested that the reason may have its roots in an embarrassing situation that Freud experienced with a hypnotized female patient. But who knows? Freud's belated admission, towards the end of his career, that hypnosis might prove to be a useful aid in therapy, could not fully redress the damage to his earlier condemnation.

Hypnosis had a rather desultory history over the next fifty years. During World War I the Germans, when their stocks of chemical anaesthetics were exhausted, reverted to hypnosis for pain control. Another application for hypnosis, both during and after the war, was in the treatment of shell-shock victims. Thousands of soldiers whose mental and emotional controls had been shattered by the terrifying horrors of war were helped through hypnosis.

In addition, there were a few tough-minded individuals, mainly in the universities, who persisted in the study of hypnosis. Notable amongst these was the American psychologist, Clark Hull, from Yale University, whose 1933 book, *Hypnosis and Suggestibility*, along with his personal influence, inspired and encouraged the future generation of students of hypnosis.

As a result of World War II and the Korean war, hypnosis and hypnotherapy was again widely used for pain control and to aid the recovery of the mentally-crippled victims of war. By the 1950s, a new interest was being expressed in the medical uses of hypnosis. In 1955 and 1958 the British and American Medical Associations studied and approved the use of hypnosis by their members provided they were properly qualified and followed specific indications for its use. Hypnotism had finally been legitimized by the medical profession.

In the last twenty years, the use and application of hypnosis has grown enormously. Again, there is a preponderance of medical applications. Hypnosis is used effecively for weight control. It is the most successful treatment available for giving up the smoking habit—with success rates, varying with the hypnotist, of 50-95 per cent. Alcoholism may be contained by it and over 150 medical disorders have been shown to be amenable to hypnotic control.

As an interesting example of a current use of hypnosis, Carl Simonton, a cancer radiologist and his wife, Stephanie, a psychologist, have established a Cancer Counselling and Research Centre at Fort Worth in Texas. At this centre cancer victims are treated with hypnotic techniques revolving around relaxation, suggestion and mental imagery, as an aid in their fight against the disease. In this treatment, used in conjunction with normal cancer therapy, patients are encouraged to visualize their cancers and what they think, or hope, is happening within their bodies. They are encouraged to see their white blood cells charging in, swarming over the cancer cells and finally destroying the cancer.

A study of the Simonton treatment found that patients who could develop good images survived longer than those who could not. In fact the ability of the patient to evoke a good, fighting image gave a better indication of the length of survival of that patient than a whole battery of the usual blood chemistry tests. As the authors of this study wrote: 'Blood chemistries are merely reflective of the body's current status. . . Psychological factors, on the other hand, seem to foretell or precede certain physical response patterns.'

We are interested in those psychological factors that precede the physical response. Yet we differ from other practitioners of the ancient art of hypnosis in that we are not interested in its medical application in this book. Instead we are interested in the use of hypnosis as the mediator between the psyche and the final physical response, with the sole aim of obtaining a larger response. And we confidently suggest that the larger physical response will be reflected in an improved sporting performance.

4
THE HYPNOTIC STATE

What happens inside a hypnotist's office? This question goes to the core of everything we have written to this stage. Let us not mislead you or excite you or let you develop too fine an edge to your anticipation. Nothing special happpens.

Certainly nothing that justifies the tense and nervous approach that many people have towards hypnosis. To these people a visit to a hypnotist is almost like a visit to the doctor or dentist. They know they have something wrong with them but fear the worst. . . it could be cancer or the extraction of all their teeth. Because they are anticipating the unknown, they know only the fear associated with the unknown. They sit in the waiting room in a tense and nervous state, clenching their hands, gritting their teeth, swallowing compulsively, just waiting for the unknown to overwhelm them.

Yet there should be no parallel between the dentist or doctor and their therapies with that available through hypnosis. There is no cause to fear hypnosis because, as we have shown, it is a natural extension of man's basic suggestibility using the simple tools, available to everyone, of suggestion, relaxation and imagination.

Imagine that you have suddenly decided that you would like to experience hypnosis. You simply walk in off the street to visit and be hypnotized by a professional hypnotist. The scenario which awaits you would run something like this.

You are invited to sit down and to make yourself as comfortable as possible. The hypnotist, or operator, then has a brief chat with you and here the operator has several objectives in mind. First is the desire to make you feel comfortable in his or her presence, to reassure you, that he is not a superhuman ogre out to manipulate psyches for good or ill. And it is important at this first meeting that an atmosphere of trust and rapport is established. As an aid to this, the operator will dispel some of the common misconceptions about hypnosis, explaining that you will not become dependent on hypnosis in order to see through the remaining days of your life, that the will is unaffected and that you do not fall asleep — rather you enter a super-relaxed and highly enjoyable state. In this way the subject's expectations of what occurs during hypnosis are aroused and it is well known that heightened expectations increase the susceptibility to hypnosis.

At some stage in this introductory chat the operator will ask the reason for your visit. Introducing the question in such an unobtrusive fashion that, hopefully, it doesn't upset the development of that air of expectancy. Your answer may cover any number of things: you may wish to give up smoking, you are chronically depressed or, let us imagine in your case, that you wish to correct a problem associated with sport. More specific questions follow. What aspects of your game are troubling you? How does this influence the result of any contest? Do you have any ideas on how to correct these faults?. . . Yet these questions are often only of secondary importance since many people have only a vague knowledge of their problem and their reasons for using hypnosis to correct it. At this stage the operator is merely finding a lead-in to the subject. The specific details and circumstances surrounding the problem will come out in questioning during the hypnotic session.

The operator, once satisfied that he is aware of the basic problem and satisfied that the subject is reassured about the correctness of his decision to use hypnosis in the solution, will begin the hypnotic induction.

Hypnotic induction should be viewed as a tool for narrowing consciousness. Seated in a comfortable chair, free from as many distractions as possible, the subject is encouraged to relax, to focus or narrow the consciousness on to the simple art of relaxation. Once relaxed, or hypnotized, the consciousness is then focused on to the problem at hand. Focus is the key word here and our interest is focused on that first stage. How does the operator encourage the subject to focus on the relaxation response?

The popular image of the hypnotist and the hypnotic

induction involves a Vincent Price figure, replete with neat goatee and mad gleam in the eye, seducing an innocent and beautiful maiden into his power through the simple expedient of a slowly swinging watch. Such a technique may be particularly valuable in hypnotic inductions performed by such characters upon their beautiful, innocent victims but it doesn't necessarily work for everyone. There are hundreds of variations on the hypnotic induction just as there are thousands of variations in the individual's response to hypnosis.

Subjects may be standing or seated or lying down; they may be stroked or not, stared at or not, asked to look at a swinging watch or the top of a distant tree. They may be asked to look at their thumbnail or concentrate on their breathing, but all the time the operator is attempting to confine the subject's attention to his voice, focusing on a particular object, while at the same time hearing only the soothing, relaxing voice of the hypnotist.

What are the chances of being hypnotized at first attempt? This crucial question pivots around your basic suggestibility, your ability to concentrate to a moderate degree and the skill of the hypnotist. But the skill of the hypnotist is the crux of the matter since nearly everyone — 99.9 per cent of you — is hypnotizable to some degree. A skilful hypnotist will have a number of induction techniques at his fingertips and be able to vary them to suit the needs of the individual subject. It would be foolish of the operator, for example, to have an asthmatic subject concentrating on deep breathing when that subject wants to find a cure for the asthma. Focusing on breathing, rattling those lungs, is counter-productive since the operator is continually reminding the asthmatic subject of his complaint. The effect would be to evince tension in the subject — a tension absolutely incompatible with the relaxed state the hypnotist is attempting to induce.

In addition to having a number of induction techniques at their disposal, skilled hypnotists should have the ability to swing from one to the other when it is clear that the first technique is not working. This is an art. It requires confidence and skill on the hypnotist's part. Finally they need to be able to pick the time to swing from one technique to another without unsettling the subject by the change or eroding the subject's confidence in them.

Unfortunately there are many practising hypnotists who rely solely on one or two techniques and once they have exhausted them without success they make the sombre pronouncement to the expectant subject that 'you are one of those few individuals who cannot be hypnotized'. This false statement is a simple reflection of the lack of skill and ability of that hypnotist, and not a measure of the hypnotizability of the subject.

An able hypnotist, by using a range of methods, will be able to induce hypnosis in at least 95 per cent of his subjects at the first session. By offering relaxation tapes or suggestions and inducements to practise relaxing over the following week, a good hypnotist should be able to pick up the great majority of that remaining 5 per cent in the next session. It is a simple fact that nearly everyone is hypnotizable.

Now let us return to you, the subject, comfortably seated, pleasantly expectant, waiting for the operator to begin the hypnotic induction. Your hypnotist chooses to use one of the many forms of the hand levitation technique.

'I want you to put your feet together flat on the floor and let your hands rest on your thighs, with your knees together as loose as is comfortable. There. That's right. And now I want you to look at your hands. I want you to concentrate on them very hard. I want you to try and let all other thoughts go right out of your mind, except for the fact that you are looking at your hands and listening to my voice. First of all, I want you to take particular notice of all the things that you can see in your hands. Looking very closely, you can see the very fine shape of the veins under the skin. . . you can see the shape of the fingers themselves. . . the shape of the fingernails, the knuckles, the wrinkles at the back of the knuckles.

'You may be able to see other things present in your hands that I haven't even mentioned. . . and now I want you to become aware of any feelings or sensations that you have in your hands. Take notice of them, become aware that they are taking place.

'You may be able to feel the blood circulating through the back of your hands and fingers. . . or you may not. . . but you *can* feel the warmth of your hands up against your legs.

'You can also feel the slight roughness of the texture of the cloth of your pants. . .

'And now I want you to look only at your left hand.

'Notice how still your left hand is. There is no sign of any movement in that hand, some part of it will make a very definite movement. It could be the index finger that will move. . . the middle finger. . . the ring finger. . . the little finger. . . or even your thumb. The fingers could begin to spread apart a little. . . a nerve could flicker in the back of your hand. . . or the whole hand could give a sudden start. . . or it could be just one of the individual fingers that will move. . .

'There have been several tiny movements in your hand already, but soon there will be a more definite one. . . one that you can see, one that you can feel. . . the fingers could begin to claw up a little bit. . . or you could develop a feeling of lightness in the whole of the hand. In fact as you look at that hand now, it is beginning to feel very light. . . it's becoming lighter and lighter all the time — just as light as a feather. The lighter it becomes, the more quickly it rises. . . It is beginning to rise much more quickly now, higher and higher. . . just as if your face were a great big powerful magnet, pulling your hand up higher and higher. . . Your hand is becoming so light now that it is slowly beginning to lift right up off your leg altogether.

'Your hand is slowly lifting right up off your leg altogether now, and it's going to keep on rising right up in the air until it touches your face. . . The higher it rises the lighter it becomes. . . The lighter it becomes the more quickly it rises. . . The moment your hand touches your face, your eyes will close right down, and you will drift off into a far deeper relaxed state than you have ever experienced before.

'As I count slowly from one to three that hand that is touching your face will become so heavy that it will fall right down into your lap again, and the moment it touches your lap you will become far more deeply relaxed. . . One, that hand is beginning to feel very, very heavy now, so heavy. It's beginning to droop downwards. . . Two, it's becoming heavier still now, just as if it were made of lead. . . Three, it is so heavy now that you cannot hold it up any longer. It's falling right down into your lap, and when it touches your lap you will be even far more deeply relaxed. . . '

This technique, as in all others, relies on a mixture of exaggeration — 'your hand is becoming as light as a feather' — plus simple statements that are rooted in fact — 'you can feel the warmth of your hands up against your legs' — to combine with the expectant air and the basic authority of the hypnotist to produce a suggestive pattern of relaxation.

Once the subject is deeply relaxed the operator will then apply a test. This test has a twofold purpose. First it gives some indication of the success of the induction. Secondly, it is used to deepen the trance and accurately gauge the depth of trance and increase the feelings of relaxation.

This test involves simple suggestions such as 'you cannot move your arm' or 'you cannot remember your name'. However, the test favoured by Les Cunningham is a simple test for automatic movement.

The subject's arm is grasped and swung backwards and forwards and the subject is asked to imagine that their arm is the handle of one of those old water pumps and that as the arm pumps backward and forwards, more and more relaxation is being pumped into their body. And then: 'In a moment or two I am going to let your arm go. When I let it go it will continue moving up and down on its own. . . And every time it goes up and down it relaxes you more and more — deep, deep relaxation. . .

'In a moment or two I am going to count to three. When I count three you will not be able to stop your arm from going up and down no matter how hard you try — and the harder you try to stop it from moving *after* I count to three, the faster it will go and the more deeply relaxed you will become. One. . . Two. . . Three. . . You can't stop your arm — it's impossible. The harder you try the faster it moves and it becomes even more impossible to stop it. . . And now, when I count to three, this time your arm will stop going up and down, it will fall down by your side and you will drift off into a far deeper relaxed state than you have ever been in your life before.'

And of course the suggestion that once the arm stops moving there will be a new sense of relaxation, is a statement rooted in fact. The end of any arm's exertion *is* accompanied by a sense of relief, of relaxation, which the subject *does* feel. And this feeling helps to reinforce all the earlier suggestions of relaxation.

Thus we have the hypnotic induction — a simple amalgam of fact and exaggeration, presented in a persuasive and permissive fashion by a master of suggestion.

Once hypnosis has been induced in the subject, the hypnotist will attempt to deepen the trance by using imagery which is evocative of deeper and deeper relaxation. The subject may be asked to imagine walking down a warm, pleasantly dark tunnel towards a distant light, or to imagine lying, hot and drowsy, on a beach or descending on a long flight of escalators and with each floor that they pass they become even more relaxed. It doesn't matter what tale is related, the key lies in inducing the subject to imagine what is a highly relaxing scene.

The words: 'I want you to imagine . . .' are the most important words in the hypnotist's vocabulary. They are key words because they place the onus on the subject to develop the session and, in this sense, all hypnosis is self-hypnosis because every subject draws upon their innate capacities for imagination and self-relaxation — the hypnotist is really only a skilful guide who picks a neat path through our capacity for imagining, helping the subject to achieve the goal of total relaxation.

Once subjects are in a totally relaxed state, their capacity to absorb and act upon *any* suggestion increases immeasurably. For example, a subject may be told that a glass of vinegar is a glass of the finest champagne and he would drink it lustily, possibly proclaiming it to be one of the finest vintages he has ever tasted. If it was then suggested that the one glass of vinegar-champagne had made him drunk, the subject would slur his words and be unable to walk in a straight line. If this line of suggestion was pushed even further: 'you have just drunk that glass of champagne and it is the most potent alcohol you have ever drunk. . . and now you are as drunk as you have ever been in you life. . .' The nausea, vomiting and any other symptoms of alcoholic poisoning could be induced in the hapless subject.

As a more refined example of the powers of hypnotic suggestion, the subject could be told that he has drunk this glass of champagne at a glittering, star-studded reception and that now it is time to go home. He is asked to picture the scene: passing from the brightly-lit reception room out into a dark and moonless night, his eyes take some time to adjust to the change in light, and our subject can now distinguish his car, parked in that dark alley-way. A measure of the subject's response to this suggestion would be seen as the pupils of the eyes dilate to take in the limited light available in that imaginary dark alley.

Examples of the power of hypnotic suggestion are many and varied and often defy imagination. Some are weird, providing such powerful examples of the capacity of the human body, that they reinforce the public's suspicion that the supernatural is invoked. People can be induced to suffer no pain when stabbed with a pin and people with normal vision can be induced to act as though they are colour-blind — seeing shades of red and green as a grey monotone.

As a further example, consider the experience of Les Cunningham, who hypnotized a very suggestible subject as part of a promotion by a New Zealand department store. This individual was led to believe that he was Rip Van Winkel and he was asleep for two days and two nights in a shop window. When Cunningham observed customers in the store pinching the subject, trying to talk to him, give him suggestions — one woman even stuck a hatpin into his arm to try to awaken him — he gave him the suggestion that from now on the only voice he would obey was Cunningham's and, if anyone else touched him or talked to him, the only effect it would have upon him, would be to make him even more deeply relaxed.

Impossible! You may well exclaim. How can such a simple routine of relaxation and suggestion produce such profound changes in behaviour? Here we come to the nub of hypnosis.

There have been many explanations of the phenomenon of hypnosis; yet these are not so much theories as points of view. One view of hypnosis insists that imagination and concentration on what the hypnotist suggests, and the tendency of such an imagination to act out the suggestion, is important. A further view is that hypnosis is a condition of mono-motivation. Another view states that hypnosis is basically role-playing. Another emphasizes the phenomenon of dissociation — a psychiatric term which is used to describe the splitting-off of one or a group of ideas from the main body of the personality, ideas which are outside conscious control. Still another view stresses that hypnosis is a regression to a childish relationship with a parent. There is truth in all these statements. But these are mere points of view or descriptions of the hypnotic phenomenon and do not provide a satisfactory insight to the workings of hypnosis and its capacity to manipulate human action.

Some of the above points of view are old, some new. However, the main theoretical controversy, a controversy which has dominated arguments about hypnosis for the past twenty years, is the question of whether hypnosis is really different from every day experience in our normal state.

Is the trance state something special, a jump, a transformation of our normal selves? Seeing it as an extraordinary condition certainly helps to explain all the weird and wonderful hypnotic phenomena. Unfortunately it is difficult to prove that this is the case. That hypnosis is in fact nothing special and not separated from reality of our daily living is a lot easier to prove.

The theory that there is nothing special about hypnosis would appear to agree with the answer we gave to the question at the beginning of this chapter. However, in that case we were referring to the induction of hypnosis, not the phenomena that flow from it.

The theory that there is nothing special about hypnosis — that the mere mention of 'hypnosis' elicits certain expectations, certain responses, a certain role-playing — has been thoroughly tested. Experiment after experiment, performed by the greatest purveyor of this theory, T. X. Barber, *seems* to show that every phenomenon claimed by hypnosis is, in reality, easily played out in our normal waking lives. These experiments have used simple suggestion on waking subjects, to duplicate hypnotic phenomena.

However it is our view that this theory does not provide an explanation of hypnosis but, rather, attempts to explain it away. Certainly, many of the phenomena associated with hypnosis can surface in normal life, but the crucial difference is the *ease* with which such phenomena can be induced by the use of hypnosis.

And this huge difference in the ease with which certain phenomena can be perpetrated, is what should concern us here. Hypnotic induction should be seen as a tool that facilitates certain unusual phenomena. If, in our normal waking state, we are asked to be drunk on a glass of vinegar, dilate our pupils, become colour-blind, ignore the pain of the surgeon's knife or stand for 48 hours in a department store window — we can do it, but it requires an almost grotesque effort of concentration and willpower. However the intervention and imaginings associated with hypnosis makes the achievement of such 'feats' commonplace.

As in so many other areas of controversy, when disparate theories are competing for attention and recognition, the true story often lies at the centre. Our view of hypnosis takes in this middle ground.

In the process of the hypnotic induction, the persuasive mixture of fact and exaggeration alters the subject's perception of reality. When a subject staring, unblinking, at a swinging watch, is told that his eyes are growing tired and want to close, it is the truth. It is a physiological fact that concentrating or staring at an object, held slightly above eye level, induces fatigue in the eyes. And when the eyes do close — through simple fatigue combined with the hypnotist's persistent suggestion — confirming the truth of the hypnotist's words — the authority of that hypnotist can only be enhanced. Similarly, in the hand levitation technique, it is very difficult for the subject to maintain a perfectly still hand. The fact that twitches or little shifts in the position of the hand do occur again fulfills the expectations aroused by the hypnotist, whose persistent suggestions become even more persuasive and authoritative.

The frequent requests to 'take a deep breath and when you do you will become even more relaxed' is also based on a physiological fact. In this case, the physiological response flows from the higher oxygen levels introduced into the blood by the deep breathing. This condition, known as hyperventilation, tends to cause constriction of the blood vessels servicing the brain and the physiological response is a feeling of wooziness or mental confusion which the subject associates with the relaxation response.

And this conglomeration of fact, exaggeration and physiological response so alters the subject's perceptions of reality that they tend to flow with every suggestion the hypnotist proffers. When the trance is deepened, through the use of highly relaxing images, the subject continues to flow with those images, eventually entering a state of super-relaxation.

And let us not understate the importance of this. The cultivation of relaxation is the crux of hypnosis. All those injunctions to relax, to go 'deeper and deeper' have parallels associated with the soothing feelings of water. Have you ever seen the action of water therapy on a distraught child? A refractory toddler is easily soothed by being allowed to play with a running tap. Water is soothing because both child and adult associate water with the most relaxed state they have ever experienced—immersion in the amniotic fluids of mother's womb. The suggestion to go deeper and deeper, to go for a ride down an escalator, to take a walk down a pleasantly warm tunnel, is unconsciously designed to recapture the insensible, passive and completely secure environment of the womb.

Insensible and passive are the key words here and although they don't do justice to the feelings of relaxation, they are adequate descriptions of brain function during hypnosis.

Brain function, and thus our bodily functions, is built around our conscious and subconscious minds. The conscious mind has the important role in our day-to-day functioning since it is responsible for assessing all the stimuli which bombard our senses in every waking moment. It chooses to filter out those which it considers to be unimportant and to hold others in abeyance while some receive top priority for action. This is our conscious mind—it is the 'I', the ever present, constantly active, constantly questioning 'I'.

In contrast our subconscious mind is exactly that—hidden to the extent that we don't know how it functions or its influence on our lives. But it is there and working, mapping out the broad strategy within which our conscious mind operates. The subconscious mind should be looked at as a mirror, but we go too fast. . .

Probably the best way to describe the subconscious is as a sink which collects every drop of information which impinges on our conscious mind. And although our conscious mind may filter out much superfluous information our subconscious mind doesn't. Because it is not as concerned with the presentation of 'I' to the outside world, the subconscious mind is there to gather all sorts of information that our various senses care to collect. Thus we can glance at a book—barely skimming the pages—but at some time in the future we may have some use for that information and we can somehow draw upon it, tapping the mysterious powers of our subconscious mind. And these powers are not confined to the collection of information. A word, a statement, a totally random event — a piece of music, a smell, a bright summer's day — can evoke a memory which we don't really understand. The basis of that memory is locked away in our subconscious, and it has the capacity to evoke and recreate those events and memories of our past.

Amidst a plethora of useless, and sometimes useful, information, we build up our subconscious mind. This should be considered to be the true 'I', because from our very first waking day it has been recording our successes and failures, emotions and feelings — the praise and admonitions of our friends and family. The synthesis of this huge amount of information provides us with our self-image.

Our subconscious mind, our true 'I' determines how we see ourselves and our every action tends to conform to and confirm our ideas of self-image. And we work out these ideas of self-image through the functionings of the conscious mind. The subconscious sets the broad strategy while the conscious is simply the tool for our every day living.

As an example of confirming and conforming to our ideas of self-image, think of an athlete who is renowned as a pressure player. In the past this athlete — through careful coaching, sheer chance or necessity — has played against all odds to win. The pleasant euphoria of victory is etched into that athlete's subconscious but an even more important influence are the emotions and feelings leading up to that important victory. In future 'pressure' contests that athlete *subconsciously* draws upon that range of emotions and feelings to recreate the optimum arousal level (the 'cool') and will to win which has served him so well in the past. The old adage that success begets success is true, and all the psychological components of success are locked into the subconscious and lie there available for creative use.

In contrast, consider those players who 'tense-up' or 'choke' at the crucial stage in a contest. These athletes' previous experiences have been failures under pressure. Possibly they were playing too hard (or were over-aroused), playing for the wrong reason or even allowing themselves to be distracted by a small incident in the crowd. Whatever the reason, they play those final, crucial points at a fault-ridden arousal level. If these experiences are repeated a number of times, those athletes become conditioned to the miserable idea that they cannot take 'the pressure' and of course they never do. They invariably choke. The broad strategy etched in their subconscious is a strategy which dictates failure under pressure.

If these examples seem a little far-fetched, consider the actions involved in catching a ball.

In the newborn state we had absolutely no idea of the concept of ball, throwing or catching. However over the years we gooed and gaahed and rolled a ball along the floor and then tripped and stumbled as we attempted to catch a bouncing ball that our father threw. And through years of practice with family and friends we slowly developed the capacity to co-ordinate hand and eye in the simple art of ball catching. But stop for a minute and think of the actions involved in co-ordinating that hand and eye.

The eye must note the speed, direction and trajectory of the ball and then feed this information to the brain. The brain must then make some decisions about the gross positioning of the body. Should the legs be moved or the torso twisted in order to line up the ball better? What is the best position for the hands? As the final impact of ball and hands approaches, the brain must then do the fine processing which will co-ordinate the twenty-odd major muscle groups in each arm plus the thousands of other fine muscles to produce the successful catch.

Now it would be possible to build and programme a ball-catching machine using techniques developed for use in, for example, a guided missile. But that machine would never be able to function at the same level of the human hand and eye. Our human ball catcher does not function like a machine, the programmes etched into that subconscious provide an almost automatic response but there is also a far from machine-like flexibility which allows him to deal with novel situations. Thus he does not say to himself: 'I will contract my deltoides muscle while extending my brachialis. . . ' because these muscular processes have been learnt. This learning process has involved negative feedback — seen in a dropped catch — and positive feedback — a successful catch with the reinforcing praise of a parent or coach. And through this feedback, practise, trial and error, the mechanism to produce a successful catch is etched or conditioned into the subconscious mind. The broad strategy provided by the subconscious dictates which muscles to use — both in position and order. Our conscious mind simply picks out the goal, a ball in flight, and feeds this information to the subconscious. The resulting strategy functions automatically and the conscious mind works out the fine control — the tactics — to achieve the goal of a successful catch.

Throughout our lives we have collected innumerable etchings which dictate our future behaviour. These etchings can relate to catching or hitting a ball, mixing with the opposite sex or handling authority figures such as policemen or referees. Our conscious mind, our waking selves, 'I', is a product of the goals and aspirations etched into the subconscious.

In hypnosis, when the subject is in a state of super-relaxation, the impact of the conscious mind is reduced to an absolute minimum and cannot interfere with, or filter out, any of the information which is being fed to the subconscious. New etchings, new patterns of behaviour, can be carved into that relaxed and susceptible mind through the technique of imagining.

As we mentioned before, the most important words in the hypnotist's armoury are 'I want you to imagine. . . ' The words that follow this request are so effective in inducing new behaviour patterns or various hypnotic phenomena because the subconscious mind is incapable of distinguishing between reality and fantasy — it accepts all 'imaginings' or suggestions as reality and a new pattern of behaviour is etched in that subconscious.

In practical terms this means that if a champion baseball catcher is hypnotized and then asked to imagine that he cannot focus on the ball ('Your vision of the ball is hazy. It seems to you that it is constantly dissolving and merging into all the white shades around it — the clouds above, the white seats. . .') and if he is asked to imagine that his arms are like rubber, flopping, stretching uncontrollably, incapable of taking any catch — then that champion catcher will fumble and drop even the most simple of catches. He will function like a two-year-old because those suggestions dominate the functioning of the subconscious mind. And all the carefully learnt skills of catching, etched in that subconscious, take second place to the more immediate suggestions that he cannot focus on the ball and that his arms are made of rubber.

On the reverse side of that coin, the same catcher may be asked to imagine a baseball, seeing the seams, the stitching, even the grains of dirt picked up in its travels—'and you see it perfectly, even when it is flying off the bat straight at you. You can still see the stitching, the colour—because you have a perfect vision of that ball. . . and now I want you to imagine. . .' If our catcher then sees himself on the playing field anticipating perfectly every ball that comes his way, with cat-like reflexes and reactions putting him in position for a successful catch, if these imaginings are further embellished by suggestions to remember the mood and experience of taking some of the most difficult and match-winning catches of his career—then he would perform to that previous standard and pull down some of the most difficult balls he has ever faced. This success arises because he has been asked to recreate the successful mood already locked into the subconscious. In addition, his subconscious has had that basic pattern of focusing on, anticipating and reacting to the ball reinforced through suggestion and imagination. Our catcher has been primed for success by placing all those behavioural patterns that relate to ball catching on a red alert.

The above examples are taken from a real sporting context, but what about the stranger hypnotic phenomena involved in making an otherwise sensible person stand in a shop window for 48 hours or taste vinegar as champagne?

In the sporting examples, the hypnotist has some real-life events to play with and all he does is recreate and embellish roles and patterns of behaviour already present in the subconscious. In the case of the shopfront dummy or the vinegar connoiseur, these individuals have no experience of acting out those roles so it is up to the skill of the hypnotist (note that we deliberately avoid the use of the term 'power') to induce the subject to imagine a new pattern of behaviour and see that pattern etched into the subject's subconscious. Once that new programme is available for use it requires no great stretch of the imagination to accept that vinegar *is* champagne or that we are Rip Van Winkel in a shopfront window in New Zealand.

This is what happens during hypnosis. There is nothing special in the hypnotist's technique and nothing special in the phenomenon: it is basically relaxation followed by skilful programming of that very personal computer, the subconscious mind. And as in any computer, the power and the uses of that computer are captive to the programmes available in its memory bank. For a finer appreciation of the skill involved in preparing that programme, we must now take a closer look at two important subjects, the development of self-image and suggestion — essential elements in the development of a successful programme.

5
A CASE STUDY IN FOOTBALL

Imagine two marauding hordes, each full of aggressive spirit. They are charging towards one another, trying to steer a leather ball through any gaps that may appear in the opposing horde's wall. A basic description of the game of rugby league; one of the many varieties of football. The game places a premium on physical fitness and aggression but, as in every sport, tactics and psychological preparation are essential inputs for any winning team.

The rugby league team, comprising thirteen members, is built around six forwards who are expected to make up the first line of defence while in attack they generally have the first taste of the ball, running it out and setting up play so that the speedier backs can take over and, hopefully, cross the opposing side's line to touch down and score a try. This is a simple description of play and in reality there is a great deal of interchange in the roles, with every player required to participate in both attack and defence at some time during the course of a game. And with the natural variation in player ability, we find that burly forwards can be strong attacking players capable of making 'breaks' through their own initiative. Similarly backline players can be strong defenders and are often in demand by coaches in order to bottle up a strong attacking opposition.

The toughest rugby league arena in the world is centred in the Sydney premiership contest, played over the winter months. The game in Sydney has reached a fine art with all the frills of modern coaching — video recorders, detailed statistics on tackling and ball distribution, and elaborate game plans. Tough physical conditioning throughout the year ensures that each team-member can play his role in the coach's game plan.

Modern sports medicine clinics help in a speedy recovery if players are injured in the process.

It is, however, becoming increasingly apparent to the top coaches that tough physical conditioning and sound tactics are just not enough. Any coach can drill his team until they reach a fine physical peak and there are many coaches adept at analysing the opposing team's strengths and weaknesses. Ambitious coaches are now looking more closely at the problem of player and team psychology.

How a coach develops and conditions the individual and team into a winning frame of mind varies enormously. Obviously some coaches have a natural flair for the task, while others contrive or conspire to influence their teams.

Some coaches have a quiet unobtrusive approach, counselling individual players during training sessions and just prior to the game. They have adopted a fatherly role, a role which emphasizes that someone cares about the players and the team; someone for whom the players will give 'their all', unconsciously seeking fatherly approval.

Other coaches use the 'fire-and-brimstone' approach epitomized in the media images of the great American gridiron coach, Knute Rockne, where appeals to family, friends and country are mixed with simple injunctions to 'kill 'em' — 'em', of course being the opposing team. This approach is often successful but Knute Rockne, in fact, hardly ever used it. The media have glamorized the myth of Rockne's successful coaching run. As a result, far too many coaches are slavish adherents of this image, believing that a vigorous pep-talk is all that is needed to motivate their players. This has three possible consequences. One is that it becomes boring and the players simply do not respond. The second is that the coach will often fire their young charges up so much that they take the injunction to 'kill 'em' literally and rush onto the field and commit an illegality. For this transgression the player may be penalized — possibly giving the opposition a scoring opportunity — or sent from the field; the team is then minus one key player or down several points. A third consideration is that some of the players may be so susceptible to the injunctions to kill 'for King and Country' that they are aroused beyond their optimum performance level.

A final point about the 'fire-and-brimstone' approach is that it requires careful preparation and conditioning. Each player must know exactly what is required of him in the game-plan and must have confidence in his own ability to play to that plan. Then and only then can he be topped with a bit of 'fire'. This careful preparation converts what could be self-defeating, wanton aggression into controlled aggression.

Another successful means of preparing players involves the conscious development of a team image. An example is provided by Roy Masters, coach of the successful Western Suburbs team, who has developed a strong team image which is rooted in the backgrounds of the players and the team. This image is that of 'battlers' — a team of battlers from a poor club, in a working class area, battling against all the odds to defeat richer, more glamorous team. It works. The Western Suburbs team is a hard-working, grinding, full-frontal bunch of successful battlers.

Similar attempts to develop a team spirit involve arranging the players in a circle and holding hands. They are then instructed to concentrate on the men next to them and told that the accumulation of energy will be reflected in the perfect functioning of the team unit once they hit the field.

It is difficult to classify Malcolm Clift, ex-coach of the Canterbury-Bankstown team. Clift had participated in and supervised one of the most successful coaching eras in the history of the Canterbury club. First joining Caterbury as third-grade coach in 1968, Clift was the first-grade coach for five years and his team always made the semi-finals. In 1975, 1976 and 1977, Clift called upon Les Cunningham to assist the club at crucial stages in the competition.

Clift is an introspective sort of father figure who carefully prepares detailed analyses of the opposing team's tactics and then develops his team to provide the winning answer. He counsels and corrects the faults in his players by judicious use of video recordings; the players respect him. Clift was also instrumental in changing the nickname of the Canterbury side from 'Berries' to 'Bulldogs' — a change in image which meshed precisely with the dogged play which Clift cultivated.

Although Cunningham's intervention has been consistently successful, we should stress that he was always called in at the last moment, though psychological conditioning for competition should be treated as a long-term venture. Such plans need to be integrated into the pre-season training schedules and developed more specifically as the season progresses. Every coach would recognize that it's better to light a fire under his charges in the early rounds of a competition and establish a clear lead which the other clubs have to peg back, rather than, in a final do-or-die effort, attempt to light a match under a disjointed and often undisciplined group of losers. This was emphasized when Cunningham was called in to help the Penrith team in 1975. The team had lost nine games in a row but after one week of Cunningham's intervention they started on a five-straight winning sequence. However, by this time, it was too late for them to gain enough points to qualify for the semi-finals.

In any case Cunningham was always called in to be the arsonist amongst a group of losing players and we will deal in detail with the lessons to be learnt from his experiences with the Canterbury side in 1977.

The season promised to be a big one for the Bulldogs. Initially well down in the betting, a successful series of pre-season games saw them established at 5:2 and equal favourites to win the premiership shield that year. The course the Canterbury side travelled during that year provides deep insight into the rigours of high-level competition and the waxing and waning of a team's mood.

In the first eight weeks of the competition their rugged defensive style of play ground out a neat path towards the premiership. Bottling up the opposing attack with their full-blooded defence, the team relied on two players — Bob McCarthy, captain and second-row forward, and Steve Mortimer, a young, live-wire attacking half-back — to spark the attack and get the winning points on the board. Over those eight weeks the Bulldogs won five games, drew one and lost two by the margin of a few points. At this stage things began to go wrong.

It is difficult to pinpoint a reason for the decline. The team had suffered a worrisome catalogue of injuries, due simply to the extremely physical pattern of their play; indeed the accumulation of injuries throughout the season concluded in a depressing end-of-year statistic: of the 16 contracted, potential first-grade players, none played more than nine of the 22 games scheduled for that season. Another reason for their sudden decline may be tied to the fluctuating performance of their brilliant half-back, Steve Mortimer.

Mortimer, at the tender age of twenty, was in his second season with the Bulldogs. In those first eight weeks of the 1977 season his brilliant, innovative attacking style earned him many column inches of compliments — 'another dazzling Mortimer display', 'the best attacking half, simply brilliant', 'the best drawcard for years'. Press headlines were reflected in the decision of the selectors responsible for preparing an Australian side, to meet a team from New Zealand, to include Mortimer in the Sydney City Firsts team that was to play a team composed of country players. In choosing Mortimer the selectors relegated Mortimer's main rival for the Australian half-back position, Tom Raudonokis, to the City Seconds side. Raudonokis, the burly and experienced twenty-eight-year old half-back for the 'battling' Western Suburbs team did not take the situation lightly. He had been Australia's No. 1 half-back for years and relished the competition from young upstarts for his spot in the national side. Newspaper banners trumpeting Mortimer's selection as A STAR IS BORN provided an exquisite challenge for Raudonikis.

In murky, rainy conditions, not conducive to attacking football, the City Firsts team asserted its usual superiority and beat the Country Firsts team by 36-0, crossing the Country line eight times in the process. Mortimer played well, crossing once himself and playing a leading role in four of the other point-scoring forays. Yet Raudonikis also had a solid game in the City Seconds win and, when the New South Wales side was chosen for the two Brisbane matches against Queensland, a series which traditionally decides the composition of the Australian side, both Mortimer and Raudonikis were chosen.

Raudonikis played in the first match. In heavy rain and with the New South Wales side short on possession, he played soundly and made the most of his limited opportunities in the team's 19-3 win over Queensland. In the return match, and with Raudonikis breathing down his neck Mortimer played atrociously. According to Malcolm Clift words had been exchanged between the two; Mortimer was 'bluffed-out', and he was feeling inferior even before he ran on to the field.

Tense, nervous, dropping the ball, running into players, Mortimer was replaced early in the second half of a particularly

violent game by the more experienced Raudonikis. Coming on
when the score was 2-13 against New South Wales, Raudonikis
changed the whole complexion of the game. He so inspired the
New South Wales side that every commentator considered it to
be his just deserts when he scored the try that gave New South
Wales its 14-13 win.

Some days later, Mortimer spoke about his rivalry with
Raudonikis: 'Looking back I can't help feeling that he psyched
me out of having a good match. . . He's an old pro and took
advantage of the situation on Sunday. A bit of stick was
required to change the trend of the game and he was the player
to inject it.'

These reflections give no indication of the depths of dejection
that Mortimer must have felt after his replacement. Quite
simply, he was shattered and wept in the dressing room after
the match. A comment he made, nearly eighteen months after
the event, is a more poignant expression of the despair felt by
someone who is so close to the top, but fails the last test: 'It
broke me up. I almost had that Australian jumper in my hand.'

Raudonikis was chosen as vice-captain of the Australian side
to meet New Zealand. Mortimer was a mere memory to the
selectors.

Within the complex field of team psychology it is difficult to
gauge the effect of Steve Mortimer's disappointment on the
performance of the Canterbury side. Quite possibly the decline
in the Bulldog's play was due to a run of injuries which were
simply coincidental with Mortimer's failure. But this is
unlikely. It should be remembered that the Bulldog's game was
built around defence and there were few players within that
team who could spark the attack that was so necessary in order
to get the winning points on the board. With a run of injuries
and a constant transfer of players from third and reserve grades
into the first tea, it was only natural that the less experienced
players looked to their established team-mates for a lead.
Mortimer was one of the two players who were expected to provide that lead but, according to Clift, he 'didn't recover' from
his experience of playing for New South Wales.

A rugby league half-forward is in the prime position to
dictate play, similar to the gridiron quarter-back. Linking the
forwards and the backs, the half-back can initiate attacking
movements or participate in the defensive play. When a key

player such as Mortimer is lacking in self-confidence the effect on the team is disastrous.

This is a subjective assessment of the Canterbury decline but it is an assessment mirrored in consistent losses and echoed by the newspaper reports on the games. Whereas Mortimer had previously featured prominently in most match reports, usually under a batch of superlatives, from the time of that disastrous game, his name hardly appeared.

The Canterbury side lapsed into a jaded pattern play, going through the motions, playing as they expected to play, not initiating, but waiting for the game to come to them. And they lost consistently.

Typical examples of this pattern play occurred in the second round matches against St. George and Parramatta. In their 5-2 loss to St. George, the Bulldogs blew their chance for victory, late in the second half, when one of their backs was set-up and in clear view of the line. With only the fullback to beat and supporting players on either side, waiting for the winning pass, our flying back made the simple choice of running smack-bang into the fullback — killing a certain try.

In the 18-10 loss to Parramatta, the Parramatta prop, Graham Olling, was racing towards the Canterbury corner post. Covered by four Canterbury defenders and with a teammate on the outside of him, Olling was expected to pass, since props are not expected to score tries from this position. But Olling did. He threw a deft dummy pass, which all four Canterbury defenders accepted was going to his teammate, and touched down himself.

At this stage Canterbury had lost four of their last six games and their chances of qualifying for the semi-finals were looking remote. After an easy win against the lowest-ranked club, Newtown — a game, incidentally, which was described as the worst game played that year — the Bulldogs had no better prospects for the finals. With a mounting injury toll, games against all the top sides facing them, and in the knowledge that they had to win six out of their last seven games to qualify, the Canterbury team management decided to tighten up the psyches of their players.

What do you do in this sort of situation?

Far too many coaches and players consider hypnosis to be a magic wand, warding off defeat while at the same time attracting victory. This is a fallacy. One wave of the wand, one team session, will not transform a team. However, the emergency situation which the Bulldogs found themselves in, meant that Les Cunningham had to work quickly to tighten up the team image and boost the players' self-confidence. His task was to condition and then reinforce the conditioning of a winning frame of mind. This involved close liaison with the coach and knowledge of the game of rugby league. In this respect Canterbury was fortunate since Cunningham had been a successful rugby league player and had a detailed knowledge of the needs of the players and the team.

As he surveyed his team in this his final coaching season, Malcolm Clift was beginning to think that he would finish this season in the same fashion as his first season of coaching with Canterbury — by just missing out on the semi-finals. It was not an appealing prospect but he had to face the facts.

Eleven of Canterbury's top players were sidelined through injury and many of the other available players were carrying minor injuries. The team was disjointed and lethargic. With the game against their main rival for the semi-final spot, Manly, scheduled for the Sunday, the outlook was not bright. Manly (the Sea-Eagles, formerly the Sea-Gulls) were in top form and at full strength for this vital game.

Clift viewed video film of the previous weekend's games of both Manly and Canterbury and examined his team's injuries on the Monday and Tuesday nights. By the Tuesday evening he had formulated a basic game plan and worked out specific roles for his players. These notes were passed on to Cunningham that evening and it was arranged that each team-member would pay a visit to Cunningham's clinic on either the Wednesday or Thursday.

Cunningham's game plan was to hypnotize the players individually and then have another session with the team about one hour before the game. He would then hand over the reins to Clift, while the players were still under hypnosis, and Clift would give his final instructions. Cunningham would then have the players for the last five to ten minutes before they took to the field, and at half-time he would have a final stamina-boosting session to help the players see out the second half.

In the game of rugby league the level of arousal needs to be very high for optimum performance. This is a fact based on the general dictum that, within a sporting context, the more complex the task the lower the level of arousal required and, conversely, the simpler the task, the higher the level of arousal that is required for optimum performance. When an athlete is co-ordinating his muscles in a delicate sporting activity, a high level of arousal is counter-productive — the adrenalin coursing through the veins will tend to make the large muscles predominant, ruining the fine co-ordination and interplay between large and small muscles.

However, in rugby league with its emphasis on simple motor skills, with the large muscles pumping, propping and co-ordinating all the body movements, you can virtually forget about the small muscles and allow the adrenalin to surge and energize all those gross muscles to a point just one or two degrees short of plain anger (see Table, p. 89). *But* the adrenalin must not be allowed to dominate; the aggression, the anger, must be controlled. Once a player slips into the arena of plain anger he loses all of his carefully learned sporting skills. And the sporting skill must always be dominant.

Those thoughts were dominant in Cunningham's approach to psyching-up the Bulldogs.

For the individual sessions Clift had prepared specific instructions for each player plus a set of general instructions which he wanted observed. To all of these Cunningham added a few suggestions, based on his own experiences, all wrapped up in the twinkling patter of hypnotic suggestion. The instructions have been numbered to show how they were incorporated into the spiel:

'Now then D, I want you to take a deep breath. . . that's good — you are relaxing more and more. . . deeper and deeper. . . And now I want you to imagine the game on Sunday: the crowded stands, the green grass, the white field markings. Can you see it? That's good. . . and now you see the brilliant blue and white colours of your team clashing with the maroon and white of the Manly team.

'And now I want you to imagine your blue and white team clashing with the maroon and white and the blue and white team is moving forward. . . grinding forward. . . all the time. . . and you are in amongst them and you have eyes only for the Manly try line and you never look backwards. . . even when a penalty kick has been awarded you don't turn your back on the ball—you move backwards into position (1). All you see is that other line.

'And when you are attacking, when you are swarming towards that other try line you are always adjusting your position so that you are in the right spot to take a pass (2). . . because you only have eyes for that other try line and all you want to do is cross it. . . and when you have the ball you set your eyes on that try line and swarm towards it, running hard, running harder than you have ever run before (3), running as if they can't tackle you. . . and you are running straight, not crowding the outside players (4). . .

'And if you are tackled you are always looking to pass that ball to a teammate (5). . . you can see it happening. . . your forward movement has been stopped but in one simple, fluid movement you have passed the ball on and it keeps moving towards that other try-line. But you don't just sit there on your ass and watch that ball move away from you. No. You jump up and back-up, backing-up all the time (6). . . always ready for another pass. . . always ready to dive on any loose balls (7) and start another movement towards that other try-line. . .'

And so on in a similar vein for the defensive movement—always getting the player to focus on the ball and with an emphasis on visualizing himself playing the best game of his life.

The specific instructions varied considerably as befits the various roles and individual quirks of each player. They ranged from a simple stress on attack and defence, such as was given to Peter Mortimer (brother of Steve) where only two points were considered necessary:

Defence—be in position and you must move up quickly to cut any movement off. Don't wait to see what happens inside you.

Attack—get back real deep to give yourself every chance.

Such instructions were easily incorporated into the spiel built around the general instructions but, as could be expected, with a greater emphasis on the basics. For example: 'you will tackle better than you have ever tackled before. . . They will collapse before you because you are like a rock, always in position and ready to block off any movement. . . Remember they can't run without legs.'

More complex instructions were directed towards Steve Mortimer as befitted his pivotal role:

1 No rests in defence—you must be in position to cover defend all the time.
2 Keep up the good line kicking but never kick to Eadie (the Manly fullback).
3 In attack drop-out now and then and give the forwards a go so that you are not constantly in play and being watched by the Manly forwards.
4 *Fight* for possession around the scrum base.
5 On their 25-metre line, sixth tackle, get back deep so you can get your kick in—and remember we will be doing BLONDIES (codename for a move) this week, not BULLFROGS.
6 When receiving ball first up from the ruck, make sure you are wide and deep.

Again, a large part of Steve Mortimer's instructions could be incorporated into the general instructions, points 1,3,4 and 6 easily fitting into the rhythm of the general spiel—but this time the emphasis being changed to meet the needs of the coach and the individual player. For example, Cunningham was aware that Steve Mortimer was lacking in confidence so the spiel made a special point of emphasizing imagery around 'you are playing the best game you have ever played in your life'.

A different tack was employed in the case of the aggressive second-row forward, Steve Hage, who in previous games against Manly had received plenty of 'stick' from the Manly forwards. With Hage lacking match fitness—only recently he had returned after nine weeks on the sidelines with a serious injury—it was expected that he would again be tested by the Manly forwards. The danger here was that Hage would respond far too vigorously and be ordered off the field by the referee—a loss that could be ill-afforded.

So the first instruction to be handed down to Hage was:

1 NO, NO HEAD HIGH TACKLES — the referee and touch judges will be on the lookout for high tackles.

The second instruction was to boost his stamina:

2 Give him stamina—only returned two weeks ago after nine weeks out with injury.

Then Cunningham moved onto specifics:

3 From rucks let Norm Thomas occasionally go two-out with you first-up.

4 Make sure of your tackles — come in on run-arounds and knock the bloke over.

5 In attack either run onto the ball and pass when you break the line or else, if you take the ball standing still, use quick hands.

6 Your weight in the scrums is essential.

It was also realized that Hage may have to take over the goal-kicking duties, so he was given several positive suggestions relating to his kicking ability. In addition, Cunningham knew that he was still worried about the chance of further injury to his knee, so he was told that his knee was strong, flexing as well as ever and that there was no need to worry about it.

The instructions for the other players varied as much as the three quoted sets of instructions. But again these instructions focused on the ball — how to get it, what to do with it and how to pass it on. Other instructions passed on by Cunningham concerned tactics, basic self-confidence, stamina and the cultivation of a grim determination, as well as correction of specific faults in style, such as 'Don't go into tackles with your arms flapping around. Drive in with your shoulder.'

Cunningham finished off each session with the suggestion that, on the Saturday night before the game, they would have a deep and satisfying sleep, and while they were sleeping all their muscles, nerves and energy would be recharging so that they would awake alert and refreshed, looking forward to a big game. A final instruction was that the next time they were hypnotized they would enter an even more relaxed state than the one they were currently experiencing. And the session was wound up.

The second stage in the psychological preparation of the Canterbury team was concerned with reinforcement of the earlier messages and the final presentation of instructions on team tactics and the role of the individual players.

All this psychological and tactical reinforcement was telescoped into one session, held two hours before the game, in the boardroom of the Canterbury Leagues Club. The players were assembled and the room cleared of everyone except Clift and Cunningham. The players were seated in the comfortable executive-type chairs or asked to get themselves comfortable by lying on the floor. Cunningham then told them to close their eyes and take three deep breaths. He then employed the usual procedure to induce group hypnosis: 'As I name the parts of the body you will make a special effort to relax them just a little bit more. . .'

Once the subjects were in a suitably relaxed state Cunningham introduced Clift: 'And now Malcolm is going to run over the game and how you should play it. I want you to be alert, listening and absorbing every word because Malcolm knows what to do to win this game.'

Clift then began his final recitation:

'We have a big game today but it's no different from any other time. If you let Manly play football they are brilliant — they can throw the ball around better than any other side. But if you get up and knock them over all day they will panic and start throwing loose passes. But honestly, if you hang off them they will kill you.

'So we have to sprint up and back all day. No walking. Sprint up and back all day. . .

'I am now going to hand you back to Les, and you are going to take notice of everything he says.'

Cunningham:

'Now fellows, you've heard what Malcolm's had to say about how to win this game, and everybody here knows exactly what he has to do. From now on you are going to concentrate only on the game — on how well you feel — on how well you are going to perform and how you are going to do more than your share today. And when you go into this relaxed state in the dressing room, you'll become even more deeply relaxed than you are now — sliding quickly into a deep state of relaxation.

'And now, on the count of three, I am going to wake you and you will wake up feeling refreshed and alert, remembering everything that Malcolm and I have told you, knowing it to be true and expecting it to be true.

'One. Waking slowly. . .'

At the conclusion of the session, the players walked the short distance to their home-ground, the Belmore Sports Ground, to prepare for the match. And when they entered their dressing rooms they were confronted by signs prepared at Cunningham's behest. Signs in the toilets, signs in the showers, signs on the roof, floor, corners — anywhere where they could not be avoided. The third stage of the game preparation — arousal of the players to competition readiness — began.

The signs contained such simple messages as I FEEL GOOD, and the trite I AM THE GREATEST, through to basic football messanges such as NO SILLY MISTAKES and BACK-UP, BACK-UP, BACK-UP ALL DAY and the harder statement: THIS IS NOT A MOTHER'S MEETING YOU'RE GOING TO. IT'S A ROUGH TOUGH GAME, TREAT IT AS SUCH. They culminated in the blatant symbolism presented by a broken football with dollar bills spilling out of its torn sides and the caption: THE BALL IS A BONANZA. WE MUST HAVE IT and DIVE ON ALL LOOSE BALLS. WE MUST HAVE THE BALL.

Another sign depicted a frightened seagul, dressed in the Manly colours with a very determined Canterbury Bulldog latched onto one leg. The caption read: DON'T LET THE SEA-EAGLES TAKE OFF — OTHERWISE THEY'LL SHIT ON YOU. TAKE THEIR LEGS FROM UNDER THEM.

While the players were getting changed, Cunningham wandered around the dressing room, talking to some, whispering to others. . . He may help one player to lace-up his boots, another to adjust his shoulder pads, help with a bit of sticking plaster, joking here and there. . . constantly mixing and moving from one player to another — attempting to keep their minds on the job ahead and create a confident atmosphere and team feeling within the group. He narrowed the team's field of thought to things pertaining only to the game.

Once the team was ready, Cunningham again relaxed them and began his final delivery. Cunningham is a big man and when he is wound-up his impressive bulk is matched by an impressive demeanour and emotional delivery of the message. And Cunningham, sweating and puffing, wound-up into a 165 kilo spring, swung his gravel voice from the soft to the hard in intoning a final arousing message which appealed to the players' raw emotions:

'You fellows are going out there this afternoon to play football — not just for yourselves, but for everybody that you've ever played football with. The kids you played with when you were going to school, grade football, the ones who weren't good enough to make the team that you're in today, your fans in hospital — they've all got a stake in you. . .

New Zealand tennis star Onny Parun. Hypnotherapy helped him beat higher-seeded players in 1975 tournaments.

A natural competitor. In the 1978 Australian Indoor Tennis Championships, self-motivated Jimmy Connors didn't even know the score when leading Geoff Masters 6-0, 4-0.

'Now you've heard your coach telling you what you've gotta do. You know what everybody's got to do, everybody's got a job out there. But you're going to do more than your share to make sure that it's done properly. No loafing, backing-up all day. That's the name of the game. If somebody's in your way and the ball is rolling on the ground, dive over the top of him, but get the bastard, get that ball!'

It was basic, gut-grade psyching-up — but rugby league is a game where guts are all. The message is guts — take the fight up the middle, fight for your family, your friends, your team. The message draws upon every primitive nationalistic, territorial instinct in the players. The message compels them to defend their territory with all the guts available and since another primitive emotion lodged in the human psyche, rationalized in the heat of combat, is intoning 'attack is defence', they lay their guts on the line by invading their opponents territory, rationalizing that it is better to run over the other bastards before they run over you.

The message is adrenalin. Surging adrenalin activating, flexing, preparing those large muscles for an all-out effort.

And the Bulldogs got the message.

In a game variously described as 'heroic' and the 'most courageous performance of the 1977 season', the Bulldogs hung in there. In a torrid game, with eleven of their team-mates watching from the sideline, the Bulldogs responded to the message to lead 3-2 at half-time.

Canterbury's points came after Peter Mortimer crashed over the line to touchdown. However, the price for that one point lead was high. Mortimer suffered a heavy sprain to his right ankle in the final swerve towards that line. This injury, later diagnosed as a flake fracture and dislocation of the ankle, forced him out of the game. Similarly the huge prop-forward, Bill Noonan, caught up in a crash-tackle, was forced from the field with severe bruising to the back and hip. Some four weeks later, after the injury failed to respond to treatment, X-rays revealed that he had actually suffered fractures to three lumbar vertebrae — an injury which meant the end of the season for Noonan.

Both Peter Mortimer and Noonan were replaced, but that finished the Bulldog's quota of reserve players. When the rest of the team trooped off the field at half-time, the battle scars from this and the earlier games of the season were showing. The injury catalogue showed that over half the players would have to take the field in the second half with some form of injury. Three in particular, Mark Hughes, with suspected broken ribs, captain Bob McCarthy, with a dislocated shoulder, and Stan Cutler, the fullback, suffering from a torn hamstring, should not have returned to the field for that second half. But they had to because each team is allowed only two replacements in any match.

During that ten-minute half-time break the masseurs and strappers worked furiously to hold their charges together. Everyone who was injured was put on one side of the room for treatment while Clift held centre stage — telling them how well they'd done, what they'd done right, what they'd done wrong and what they had to do in the second-half to keep it going. . . pointing to the weaknesses he'd picked out in the Manly team. Cunningham then had the final five minutes of the break to boost the players.

Because of the time factor Cunningham condensed the hypnotic induction by using one of the very basic tests of suggestibility, asking them to close their eyes and put a hand on top of their head. . . 'and now I want you to imagine that there is a little hole there and you're looking through the top of your head at your hand. Visualize the shape of your hand, the shape of your fingers. . . the fingerprints. . . the pores of the skin. . . and keep your eyes fixed firmly on your fingers, don't take your eyes off them whatever happens. . .

'And when I count to three you will find that you can't open them. . . One. . . Two. . . Three. . . You can't open your eyes. Keep looking at your hand. . . it's impossible you can't open your eyes. . . But don't try any more — just let your hands fall down by your side and take a deep breath. . . There we go. . .

'Now you're doing fine. You're going terrific — but everything you did in the first-half you're going to do a little bit better in the second. Because now we're into the straight, we're into the final stage and we're in front and we're going to stay there. You're not going to let those bastards take anything away from you. . .

'And to do this you are going to drag out stamina you never even knew you had before. Stamina, energy, guts, will flow from out of your toenails and every other part of your body — keeping you on the go, on the ball, right through to that final whistle. . .

'You will feel as if the game has only just begun; they have thrown everything they've got at you and you are still one point in front. We are now going to increase the pace. . . putting more pressure on them than we did in the first-half. . .

'This is the most important game of our lives and we are going to do everything we've got to do to win. Minor bruising and small aches and pains we will not feel until after the game. . .your reflex action will be sharper than in the first half, your thinking will be clearer and there is nothing that Manly can say or do that will upset you and get your mind off this victory. . .'

In a tense second-half, all three of the more severely injured players had crucial roles to play. McCarthy was playing an inspirational captain's role, holding a tight defensive line up the middle, bringing down the Manly attack with simple shoulder charges. And just in case one shoulder wasn't enough, he made a point of positioning the reserve forward, Peter Cassilles, close to his weak side in order to catch any Manly players who managed to break through. Few did, despite his shoulder popping-out again and having to be forced back in.

Nine minutes into the second half, Manly's live-wire half-back, Johnny Gibbs, scuttled through the defence to touch down — a try with a converting goal which gave Manly a 7-3 lead. Malcolm Clift almost gave up the ghost at that stage, yet things started to click for the Bulldogs when a successful penalty goal reduced Manly's lead to 7-5. Manly retaliated with a brilliant attacking move which led to the Manly winger racing full-bore along the sideline and with only the crippled fullback to beat. Cutler, dredging-up a final effort — probably from under his toe-nails — was able to nail the movement and he stopped the Manly winger a few centimetres short of the Canterbury line.

In the continuing ragged interplay of attack and defence, neither side appeared ready to break until ten minues from the finish when the Canterbury winger, Greg Mullane, who had been switched to the centre three-quarter position while the injured Mark Hughes rode as a passenger on the wing, made the break.

Pushing through the Manly forwards, Mullane carved a jagged inroad through the Manly territory, gaining some 60 metres in the process. With the defence closing, Mullane passed crisply to the other centre, Mick Ryan, who set his sights on the Manly corner post. Running hard but diagonally towards the Manly line, the cover defence had time to reform and swarm around Ryan and the supporting Hughes. With the defence about to take his legs, Ryan threw a high floating pass which Hughes, at full pace and stretching to get the reach, gathered-in, only yards from the Manly line. Despite his injured ribs and two Manly defenders blocking his path, Hughes bullocked his way over to touchdown in the corner and made the score 8-7, Canterbury's way.

Hughes was carrying out goal kicking duties on the day but was too distressed through his injury to attempt the conversion of his own try. So Steve Hage took the difficult sideline kick, successfully, to stretch the lead to 10-7. A last minute penalty goal produced the final wining score of 12-7.

After the game Malcolm Clift commented to journalists: 'It was guts that got them home'.

It is obvious that the tactics used in the psychological preparation of the Bulldogs relied to a certain extent on shock. The sudden change in their game preparation and the exhortation and suggestion around the very fundamentals of the game — 'getting the ball', 'getting your man', 'running hard', 'backing-up' — was a shock to professional footballers who were more at home discussing the finer points of the game. Probably the last time they had thought so deeply about the basics was when they were playing football as juniors. This return to the roots of the game — concentrating on the ball and combining as a team — was needed to shake Canterbury out of its lethargy and provide the winning formula.

Now we turn to the Canterbury team in 1978. Malcolm Clift had retired and been replaced by Ted Glossop as coach. The Bulldogs had plugged along, not playing brilliantly, not playing badly, and had scraped into the semi-finals. Their opponent in the sudden-death, first semi-final, were the premiership favourites, Parramatta. And Parramatta were quoted as odds-on to beat Canterbury by all the bookmakers.

The focus was again on Steve Mortimer who was trying to recapture the form which won him the New South Wales jumper the previous season. Mortimer had been forced to play most of the season out of position, at five-eighth, and had an ordinary season — plugged into the Canterbury team, plugging along with it. He had not captivated any of the selectors and this was his one last chance. All three selectors, responsible for choosing the Australian team to tour England and France, were to be present at the Sydney Cricket Ground to view the Canterbury-Parramatta clash. And Mortimer had been returned to his favourite position as half-back, where he hoped to demonstrate his natural attacking flair.

According to Mortimer: 'I'm a different player to a lot of the other Canterbury players. People reckon they can't read me. One minute I'm here and the next minute I'm doing something different over there. . . and I broke my game down to just play along with the team — that's what I was doing all the year. . . and my confidence was lacking.

'I was playing out of position and could see that I wasn't firing and the team wasn't firing. I was playing OK but I was tackling more and I'm not a tackler — I'm an attacker and I thought to myself "stuff it", its not getting us very far. We got to the finals but we're better off if I just do my own thing — attack — because that's what I should be doing.'

Mortimer wanted a big game and knew he had it in him: 'I thought "this is stupid not being at the top." I wanted to get to No. 1 again and since I felt really good the other times I visited Les — I played one of the best games of my life (after seeing Cunningham) — I thought he could instil the necessary confidence in me.'

And on the Friday night before the big match, Mortimer paid a private visit to Cunningham, without telling coach or team-mates. According to Cunningham, Mortimer was 'tense and afraid of playing a bummer of a game. He wanted to play a big game before the Australian selectors and wanted some help to boost his self-confidence. . . so I covered everything. I told him he'd be on the ball and make no silly mistakes, that his reflex actions would be sharp and sure, that he would have stamina, guts and determination and think clearly all the time. I went over everything twice to make sure he played right at his top.'

Because he had had previous experience of hypnosis and had responded so positively, he was an easy subject for

Cunningham to work with, relaxing him and then reinforcing all those earlier experiences — 'Remember how well you played after you saw me last time' and 'I want you to imagine the best game you've ever played in your life. . . You can remember that 1976 experience when you played and beat the top club in the world, Eastern Suburbs, in the greatest upset of the year. . . I want you to remember how you felt.

Mortimer arrived at the SCG well before the rest of the team, already dressed. He cut himself off from the ribaldry and chiacking of his teammates and watched the reserve grade game. Although usually very tense before a game Mortimer cannot describe his feelings before the Canterbury-Parramatta clash. His feelings, his tension, fluctuated — actually a symptom of a controlled psyche preparing for a big contest, swinging through aggressive thoughts to controlled clear visions of the course of the game and the role he would be playing.

The Canterbury-Parramatta semi-final was won by the favourites, Parramatta, by 22-15. The role Steve Mortimer played in this game is best described by newspaper reports on the match: 'To win yesterday, Parramatta defied a game of absolute dazzling quality from Mortimer — a performance which would certainly have sunk just about any other side' *(Daily Telegraph)* and 'Steve Mortimer relished the return to half-back where he was free to exploit his tricks and acceleration. He was the architect of all three Canterbury tries' *(Rugby League Week)*.

The first try involved Mortimer making a small chink in the Parramatta defence then kicking deftly ahead for his winger to collect and touchdown. The second was a superbly opportunist try as Mortimer swept in to intercept and juggle a high pass between two Parramatta backs. With the entire Parramatta side in hot pursuit, Mortimer ran 90 metres to score. Five minutes later with a dummy pass and big side-step, he beat half-a-dozen would-be Parramatta tacklers to touch down again.

A brilliant individual display does not always win team games but could it win him an Australian jumper? To many spectators his selection was a foregone conclusion. According to *Rubgy League Week:* 'Just forty minutes of Steve Mortimer convinced me he should be chosen in the Kangaroo (Australian) squad.

'Mortimer proved he has completely recovered from the shattering morale blow he suffered last year.

'Last year Mortimer played for New South Wales against Queensland but turned in a shocker.

'Until last Sunday he had not reproduced the form or should I say magic, that won him a State jumper.

'I rate Mortimer's display last Sunday as the most brilliant individual effort of the season. . .

'I believe Mortimer is a rugby league genius and that's not a term I hand out on a platter. . .

'I urge the Australian selectors to take him to England for the sake of the game.'

The selectors response was negative.

Mortimer had been tested in a big game before and had failed. There are to be no opportunities to learn from previous mistakes. You either have a competition mentality or you don't. A competition mentality is innate in successful footballers. It cannot be learned or imposed upon a failure through hypnosis.

A rag-bag of prejudices, but then everybody is entitled to a few and misconceptions about the use of hypnosis in sport are hardly new. To some commentators (and probably the Australian selectors) rugby league is a man's game and brawn is more important than brains. To influence the brain through hypnosis is something they don't understand and if they don't understand, then it's got to be bullshit.

Now, the influence of hypnosis or any form of psychological preparation, on the outcome of a game, especially a team game, is one of the great imponderables. The only measure you can make is a simple subjective assessment and, in an effort to balance the presentation in this chapter, we should point out that some of the Canterbury players who experienced hypnosis were sceptical of the results. They believed that Cunningham's intervention was peripheral to their eventual success and that they won through their own resources of strength, guts and will. Possibly they did, but every bookmaker every pundit, said they couldn't win in 1975, 1976 and 1977. The final points on the board reflected the value of Cunningham's intervention. And points are what count in the final analysis.

Prejudice is a deeply rooted emotion but it is about time the prejudice that strength is *all* is buried so deep that it's forgotten. Successful competition is built upon a triad of strength, tactics and careful psychological conditioning. This conditioning is often too subtle for certain sceptics to grasp. But remember, there are many examples of the success of psychology, more particularly hypnosis, in sport. The points are on the board.

6
THE PROBLEM OF THE PSYCHE-UP

Every sport has a measure of aggression: the simple conflict in the competition drama, the assertion of superiority and the final result—dominance and submission—provides a neat cycle of aggression, victory and defeat.

Now after that description of the gut-grade psyching-up of the Canterbury football team, the question arises about the psyche-up and aggression level appropriate for other sports. Not only does the level vary for different sports but there is a further complication in the individual's attitude to the sport in question. In general, most athletes need to be psyched-up but with some individuals, psyching-down or pacifying the athlete, produces a better sporting performance. It is a common fallacy that the psyche-up is open-ended—that the more intense the arousal, the better the performance. In this chapter we present a general description of aggression and arousal and the levels of arousal appropriate to various sports. First-off we should take a closer look at the phenomenon of aggression.

For a long time the word 'aggression', with its ability to conjure up visions of violence, death and destruction, has had nasty connotations. To many connoisseurs of peace, aggressive behaviour is abnormal behaviour. And to these individuals, the rousing injunctions of the previous chapter to 'tread all over them' and 'kill 'em' is direct evidence of the psychopathic nature of football. We will not debate that point here except to reiterate that while there is an aggressive component in every sport, some sports require more aggression than others, and there are available to sports psychologists and coaches a number of verbal tricks that can arouse athletes to an optimum competition level. If these verbal tricks rely on a crude collection of words then this relates back to the fact that words are very crude tools for describing states of mind. Critics of the techniques used in psyching-up football players are confusing the dictionary meanings of a collection of words with the motives behind their use.

Now although it may be anathema to some people, we have to state that aggression is a vital and quite proper emotion. Animal studies by the great ethologist, Dr Konrad Lorenz, have shown that aggression is fundamental to an animal's behaviour and that an animal cannot feel or express affection until channels have been provided for the expression of aggression. A sporting contest is a channel for ritualizing aggression and every participant, whether it be over a pool table, on a cinder track or on a roaring football field, will have a measure of adrenalin surging through their veins. And adrenalin is the key to an understanding of aggression.

The release of adrenalin from the adrenal glands, located above each kidney, produces a number of physiological effects, all familiar to anyone who has ever experienced anger or fright.

The most important and obvious effect of this is a rapid increase in blood pressure, which is caused by an increase in the rate and force of contraction of the heart and through constriction of the peripheral blood vessels. Furthermore, this increased blood flow is directed away from organs such as the kidneys and intestines and is concentrated on energizing the muscles. And, as a further aid in this energizing, adrenalin causes an increase in the blood-sugar level and enlarges the bronchial passages of the lung, allowing higher volumes of oxygen to enter the accelerated blood flow.

The total effect is energy, tension and power—exactly the qualities needed by primitive man to meet the daily emergencies of his violent existence. And that is the reason for the evolution of the adrenal gland function. It was designed to activate primitive man in an emergency situation, preparing him for the fight or, if things looked hopeless, to run like hell. This is the basis of W. B. Cannon's description of adrenalin producing the 'fight or flight' reaction.

The term 'arousal' is quite distinct from the term aggression. Arousal is built from several distinct components which interact to produce the final package. Adrenalin is just one of these inputs. The others are the sensory system and various functions and capacities of the human computer.

Basically arousal is needed to keep the body functioning and the brain is constantly trying to balance and coordinate a wealth of information to produce the best response in any given situation. In a sporting contest a wide range of information and stresses, demanding quick responses, needs to be synthesised into a winning formula — and in this situation, under or over-arousal can detract from a successful performance. It is appropriate that we now describe the process of arousal.

Arousal begins with the perception of an arousing event. Although this sounds trite it is a simple fact that perception precedes any reaction. The arousing perception may be a fierce animal or merciless enemy, but in a sporting contest it is the more prosaic view or expectations associated with the arena, crowd and opposition. And, as we have pointed out, the arousing event can simply be imagined — bad dreams are a good example — since a carefully controlled fantasy; whether it involves fear or anger, is just as effective as the real event in stimulating the arousal response.

The body perceives and experiences this initial reaction to an arousing event through the reticular formation of the brain. This part of the brain is responsible for keeping the body aroused or activated through a range of emotions extending from sleep upwards and, in this sense, is responsible for monitoring and activating a wide range of bodily movements and functions. Due to its extensive connections with other parts of the brain, once the reticular formation perceives an event as arousing, various messages are telegraphed to other parts of the brain. One distinct part of the brain which receives a message is the limbic system.

The limbic system is considered to be one of the more primitive parts of the brain with roots far back in the evolutionary past. The functions of the limbic system are a little obscure but from animal studies it seems that the limbic system functions in conjunction with the hypothalamus in the regulation of emotional and motivational responses to outside events. One half of the system seems to be involved in the development of dominant-submissive roles, while the other half seems to regulate aggressive behaviour. Such roles must be played out in conjunction with another area of the brain, the hypothalamus, because of the latter's crucial role in brain-body functioning.

The hypothalamus is the third very crucial component of the arousal process. Again the hypothalamus has very extensive connections with other parts of the brain and the nervous system as a whole. It is involved in the regulating of blood pressure, hormonal levels, intestinal activity, dilation of the pupils of the eye, heartbeat and a host of other regulatory activities including control of emotion and arousal states. It is often described as the 'centre of the emotions'.

Amongst this plethora of hypothalmic functions is the fact that the hypothalamus stimulates and controls the release of adrenalin from the adrenal gland. And we would appear to be right back where we started, with adrenalin and aggression.

However, it is a rather more complicated than that, since the cells of the reticular formation of the brain are particularly sensitive to adrenalin and thus the adrenal gland exerts some control on the initial arousal level. This is a classic example of the feedback loop — a loop which serves to regulate the arousal level through perception and response. The response producing futher perceptions which feedback and fine-tune the arousal level until the 'best' solution or response to the problem at hand is produced.

Apart from the feedback loop operating between the adrenal gland and the reticular formation, there are probably many other loops operating from the body to brain and brain to body — the relationship between the limbic system and the hypothalamus is one obvious candidate for further study. The complexity of these interactions only serves to highlight the fact that anger and fear and the 'fight or flight' reaction of adrenalin is not all there is to the aggressive component of sports. The arousal system is a complex and, to a certain extent, self-regulating process which is designed to allow the human animal to give the best physical and mental response to a perceived situation. In sport this means the best possible combination of brain and brawn.

In contrast to our primitive ancestors, we are blessed with the relative absence of emergency situations. However, if an emergency does arise, modern man is still capable of 'fight or flight' and the massive release of power that flows from that reaction. The example in the introductory chapter of the slight woman who lifted a car off her trapped son is just one of countless examples of human strength and heroism which occur in war, peace and sport.

But not every emergency situation demands a response of crude power. A bomb-disposal expert defusing a rapidly ticking time-bomb needs control, not power. Similarly, in the ultimate crunch of a team sport—one point down and five minutes left in the grand final—a huge surge of adrenalin associated with anger and the blind will to win, can be counter-productive if all control is lost.

Arousal, strength, control and performance. The inter-action between these four variables is complex and there is no straight-line relationship which says increased arousal and increased strength tips the odds in favour of success in a sporting contest. Success in sport, as in so many other fields of life, is built around the careful integration and expression of those two variable, yet crucial, inputs of quality and quantity. Let us reflect for a moment on the sporting implications of quality and quantity.

Quality is style, control and precision. In a sporting context it means the ability to play the game the correct way, the book way, the coaches' way—whether it be correct footwork and perfect strokeplay, the careful positioning of hands and arms around a dumb-bell or the perfect roll and swivel of the hips in a running race. Quality is learnt through careful coaching and dedicated practice combined with the lessons of top competition. Quality is obvious in the performance of any champion athlete.

In contrast quantity is the physical input, the very basic movement associated with every sport. It involves the three measures of strength, power and endurance—sheer muscle. Quantity is not learned; it grows from pure dedication and hard work and since it is muscle, it is particularly vulnerable to the effects of emotional arousal.

In any contest the drama of the competition always has to fluctuate around the relative merits of quantity and quality. Yet what is the contribution of each to success? Where does the balance lie?

The balance lies in reaching the optimum level of arousal; which in turn, is dictated to by the tenets of the sixty-year-old Yerkes-Dodson Law, which states that the simpler the task, the higher the level of arousal necessary for success. The corollary is that the more complex the task, the lower the level of arousal required for successful completion of that task.

Expressed graphically, with the horizontal axis of the graph recording arousal and the vertical axis performance, we would find the curve of sporting performance carving out the shape of a bell. This demonstrates that a 'low' performance can be induced by both too low and too high an arousal level. For a high arousal sport such as football (see Table, p 89), the bell would be pushed over to the right-hand-side of the arousal axis while for a low arousal sport, such as golf, the bell will hover around the left-hand-side of the graph.

Numerous studies have confirmed the validity of the Yerkes-Dodson Law. Probably one of the more sensational was a study conducted by Dr J. R. Patrick and reported in the 1934 *Journal of Comparative Psychology*. Patrick shut a subject in a cabin with four doors. The idea of the study was to see how quickly the subject could escape from the cabin when three of the four doors were locked. Of course, Patrick complicated the situation by varying the escape door.

The subjects very quickly adopted a rational strategy and found their way out. However, the motivation to escape was increased by giving light electric shocks through the floor or shooting nails at the subject. The rational approach to the problem of escaping soon fell by the wayside and the subjects' response became less rational, stereotyped but, above all, less efficient: it took them longer to escape.

In a more civilized study, Dr B. Bergstrom tested the ability of experienced airline pilots to perform a secondary task aside from their main task of piloting a plane.

Bergstrom reported that the human pilot can perform extremely complex tasks in the calm, laboratory situation of a simulated cockpit. But when the same test system is conducted air-borne and the immediate stresses of controlling the plane intrude into the pilot's thinking, the level of arousal is way above the optimum necessary for successful completion of the secondary tasks, and the test performance drops dramatically.

A more common example of the effects of over-arousal is seen in the human reaction of panic. Now a man about to be chased by murderous Indians can vent his panic by indulging the 'fight or flight' reaction and simply run. However, the panic reaction associated with, for example, a fire, where there are always some impediments or problems to be overcome, is not really compatible with blind, fast flight. Thus people will try to break down a locked door and won't think to use the key sitting in the lock. The afflicted, and soon dead, individuals do see the key but in their blind flight they cannot comprehend its use. Gross power and flight, without any thought, is the panic reaction; it involves getting as aroused as anyone will ever get in their lifetime.

The physiological reason for equally low performance at both high and low arousal levels is that at too low an arousal level, performance is hindered by inadequate attention — that stepping-off point of perception is not activated sufficiently to arouse an adequate performance. At too high an arousal level the opposite occurs: excessive attention is focused on the arousing object or event and the narrowed perception that results sees the individual miss, or not perceive, other important aspects of the arousal event.

In a sporting contest over-arousal sees the athlete forget all those carefully nurtured skills and rely instead on brute power and aggression to force a victory. Jack Johnson, the huge, black, heavyweight boxer, used to take advantage of his white opponent's various susceptibilities. During the bout he offered taunts around the theme of: 'After I've knocked you out boy, I'm going to leave you flat on your back and then I'm going to take and have your woman'. The anger associated with the possibility of black physical and sexual superiority was too much for many, and they lashed out blindly. And, as every boxer knows, the easiest target in the boxing world is an angry boxer — because in their blind desire to fight, they completely ignore the requirements of defence. A cool and controlled opponent will easily evade the crude blows and pierce an almost non-existent defence.

In football, provoking an opposing player into a rage destroys those basic dictums of 'watching the ball instead of the man' and 'playing the ball instead of the man'. In his desire to get even, the enraged player looks for the man, committing unforced errors and illegal violent play which can see him sent from the field or penalized — a situation which makes the other side's task so much easier.

Anger directed at oneself can be just as destructive as anger directed at an opponent. Players who experience frustration and anger over not playing to their own high standards — that is, they are not winning — are a common sight in any sport. In tennis, for example, the action which evokes the anger may be a simple overhead smash — the subject of intensive practice — going into the net. The anger that susceptible players feel over their failure tends to boost their arousal level way above the optimum and this heightened arousal sees the muscles take over — rushing the ball, rushing the net — chasing their anxiety to succeed all over the court until the final result is a loss in style, precision and intelligent functioning. Further failures result and so they become even more angry and failure prone. Such individuals lock themselves into a cycle of anger and failure which only serves to confirm their original assessment about how badly they are playing. Such a cycle is self-defeating.

The problem of under-arousal is just as big a problem as over-arousal. The 'lazy' player who just cannot get motivated is one example; possibly such individuals are really not interested in their sport and shouldn't be playing. However, there are cases of athletes whose arousal and performance fluctuates wildly around the bottom half of the arousal spectrum and their off or 'lazy' days are days, when, through ignorance or inexperience, they have not been successful in psyching themselves up to their optimum arousal level.

A classic example of the consequences of under-arousal concern a Czechoslovakian boxer at the 1968 Mexico Olympics whose tension and anxiety were relieved by a sports psychologist through the intervention of progressive relaxation. This relaxation was so successful that the boxer came out of his corner for the first round still smiling and carrying his arms at his side. The smile was wiped from his face after one minute and thirty seconds when he was knocked out. Here was a definite example of an athlete who needed a certain level of tension to perform properly. The psychologist simply did not take enough care in adjusting the arousal level.

Another familiar example of under-arousal is the player or team that builds up a good early lead in a contest and then, with final victory in sight, relaxes. This is usually described as a derivative of that catch-all explanation: 'loss of concentration'. Now 'loss of concentration' may arise from a number of factors — a fault in the playing area, a girl in the crowd, the antics of a team member or of the opposition — but it is essentially a distraction. The appearance of a relaxation phase in a contest arises through sheer complacency. Easy, early points seduce the winning athlete or team into

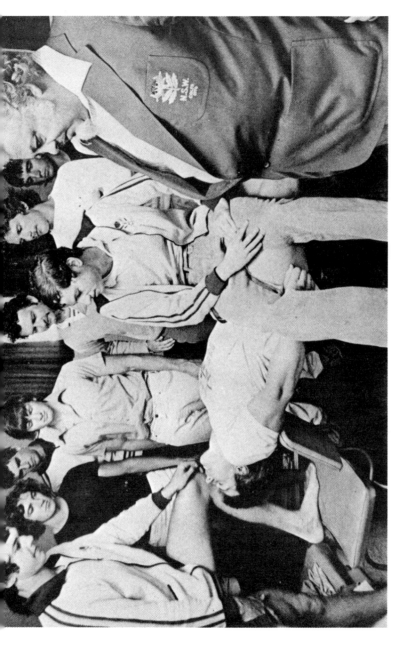

The New South Wales Colts crew, which established a world endurance rowing record, under the watchful eye of their consultant hypnotist.

underrating the opposition and, anticipating an easy victory, they unwind and in doing so unconsciously lower the arousal level which was crucial in winning those early points.

Arousal levels, with the concomitant effect on performance, can fluctuate wildly in a very short period of time. Consider the experience of Leonid Zhabotinski, a Russian weightlifter, during the 1966 World Weightlifting Championships. Weightlifting because of its emphasis on pure muscle power, is a sport where an extremely high level of arousal is essential. In Zhabotinski's case, he was facing a snatch of 160 kilograms — a relatively light weight for the man who eventually won the heavyweight division in this contest, setting a new world record in the process.

Complacent over not being fully extended, Zhabotinski underestimated the weight and failed to attain the correct arousal level. Lacking power, the snatch failed. Angry at his failure on the first attempt, Zhabotinski slipped into an over-aroused state and really 'snatched' at the weight — pulling the bar up so strongly that it flew over his head, upset his balance, and then fell behind him. Zhabotinski's 'easy' snatch was successful only on the third attempt, when he had struck a balance between under and over-arousal.

Similarly, it has been shown that during basketball games the free-throw shooting success varies with the score difference and that this appears to relate back to the arousal level of the free-thrower. For example if the score differential is only a few points, the thrower is too concerned about his success and, being over-anxious, his performance drops. When the score differential is slightly higher (say five to eight points) there is not such a crucial requirement for success but this is balanced by the fact that the match is still close and the free-thrower produces his best performance — being not too anxious but still determined. When there are large differences in the score complacency seems to set in and, not really caring, performance drops back to a level equivalent to that of the over-anxious player.

How does an athlete strike that delicate balance between anxiety on the one hand and complacency on the other, to produce his best performance? Or, in other words, how does he balance arousal and intelligent functioning so that he makes the most of the Yerkes-Dodson Law?

Most athletes strike the balance very slowly; it arrives

through trial and error, wins and losses. Others have learnt various techniques, some good, some bad — the pitcher who felt the need to whip himself up into a rage before he could perform, is one bad example. But for most of these experiments in arousing oneself the results are erratic, usually because the experimenter does not have a systematic approach to the problem.

We have already mentioned the concept of a 'competition mentality' and how many champions seem to have the ability to switch off any interest in extraneous events and focus all their attention and energies on the problem at hand. For these athletes, competition is a breeze and their psychological preparation for a contest is akin to a workman donning a pair of overalls before settling down to his work.

A competition mentality is constructed from many other inputs besides arousal. Some of these are: a very basic need to win (for whatever reason); an ability to concentrate on the game and avoid the unsettling consequences of trivial distractions; and the ability to read the direction of play and adjust tactics accordingly. Behind all the components of a competition mentality, the arousal level is continually impinging on and influencing the individual's mental progression through the contest.

If we consider the development of arousal in isolation from other aspects of the competition mentality, we eventually get back to the old axiom that success begets success. In the early years of a champion's evolution either luck, good coaching or natural ability, or a combination of all three, saw that the optimum arousal level was conceived. Victory, success, the praise of a coach, family and friends — all served to fix that feeling of competition arousal in the young champion's mind. The next contest sees our young champion attempt to duplicate those feelings to win again the praise and elation associated with victory. A very Pavlovian ritual of arousal, success and reinforcement. A very potent reinforcing cycle which, other things being equal, serves to fine-tune the arousal level and the development of that elusive competition mentality.

And, as in all types of Pavlovian ritual and reinforcement, the optimum arousal level can be learnt. To this end we have prepared a table which attempts to balance the competing ends of the Yerkes-Dodson Law. It provides an indication of the optimum arousal levels for various sports set in the arousal continuum between dead sleep and blind anger. In this table sports are placed on the scale at a point which strikes a balance between the quality and quantity components of an excellent performance. This means that those activities which place a premium on speed, strength or endurance but have a low demand for the qualities of judgement, precision and fine-muscle control are near to the top of the arousal continuum. In contrast, sports which place a high priority on judgement, fine muscle control and co-ordination but place a low priority on the need for strength, speed or endurance, appear at the lower end of the scale.

Of course many sports require a combination of the various factors which make up the quality and quantity components of performance and there a compromise has to be reached. For example, the boxer who needs the strength, speed and endurance available through high emotion must, at the same time, intelligently analyse his opponent's movements and figure out ways to capitalize on his opponent's weakness and his own strengths — all the while anticipating and protecting himself from his opponent's blows.

In running races, the highly aroused athlete about to compete in a 100-metres sprint is liable to jump the gun or be slow off the mark because a high arousal level is incompatible with a fine response to the starter's gun and valuable split-seconds can be lost. However, in longer sprints, 200 and 400 metres, the lack of a fine response to the starter's gun is easily counterbalanced by the greater benefits of speed and endurance. In long races a runner in a highly aroused state tends to throw caution to the winds, fail to pace himself, and then tires dramatically at the end of the race, so he should avoid a state of extreme excitement.

The optimum arousal level also varies within team games depending on the position of the players. Thus the rugby league halfback and the gridiron quarterback — in positions which call for the co-ordination of play — are lower on the arousal continuum than their running and tackling team mates. And it is worth pointing out that group pep talks with their emphasis on the open-ended psyche-up, are often counter-productive simply because not every player requires the same degree of arousal; the coach who practises the open-ended psyche-up philosophy stands the risk of having some of his crucial players at an inefficient and unnecessarily high level of arousal.

How does the individual athlete fine-tune his arousal level? In Chapter 10 we offer various suggestions to be used in conjunction with Chapter 11 on self-hypnosis. These suggestions, which focus on various aspects of sport, are designed to slot into the self-suggestion phase of hypnosis and the subject is encouraged to imagine himself playing the correct strokes, seeing the ball clearly and reacting promptly and properly, or running fast and freely. Such images are translated into reality during the next contest and the arousal level appropriate to that activity develops as those imaginings are acted out. But this tells us little about fine-tuning the arousal level and to achieve this the athlete must establish a baseline to work from.

The table of arousal levels presented in this chapter is only a crude guide to the optimum arousal level for each individual — for the individual the best approach is to incorporate into the self-hypnosis sessions, images and memories of the best game he has ever played in his life. This is the best approach because we can say with some certainty that, during that particular 'best ever' game, the arousal level of that individual must have been pretty close to the optimum. Memories and images of the best ever game should be carefully cultivated in an attempt to fix the feelings associated with that game in the subconscious mind.

Whether success or failure follows the use of this technique, the feelings associated with the game and the course of the game, should be carefully analysed. Any loss should be thought out in terms of whether you were under or over-aroused and an adjustment, through varying the arousing images, should be made before the next contest. When victory follows an experiment in arousing yourself, immediately afterwards you should try to recall how you felt before the start of the contest and the elation of victory. Relax yourself, lie back and remember—imprinting those feelings in your subconscious mind for future reference. Probably the best way to fix those feelings is to associate a few words and/or a colour with the memories of arousal and victory. These words and colours can then be recalled and used to adjust your arousal levels before future contests. Examples of such key words and colours are descriptions such as 'a fine rage' and 'cool and detached'. These words can be associated with colours — red representing the upper end of the arousal spectrum and blue the cooler more controlled state.

Refine the use of these key words or colours by integrating them into an arousing ritual in the warm-up period before a contest. Go through the same procedure before every contest. In tennis, say, take off your watch, do a few knee bends and touch toes, arrange your towel neatly, all the while thinking of your words and colours. Then, still thinking of these words and colours, start hitting-up. Before a running race, do a few exercises and some short sprints then remove your track suit and arrange it perfectly, the same way, every time. Again be thinking of your key words and colours.

All of this is simply a variation on the continual, and often boring, injunctions of coaches, to 'warm-up properly' before a contest. But warming-up muscles and limbs is only of secondary importance in the coach's ritual. The real purpose of such a ritual — no matter how trivial or time-wasting it may seem — is to cue you into the arousal state necessary for competition. Like Pavolv's dogs, the constant repetition of the ritual (the bell), the cultivation of the arousal response (salivation) and the reward (food) — or in your case a contest victory — helps in the development of the arousal state to the optimum level appropriate for you.

OPTIMUM AROUSAL LEVELS FOR A RANGE OF SPORTS		
Arousal Level	Description	Sporting Activity
10	Blind panic or anger	
9	Extreme excitement	Rugby league and rugby union (forwards)
8		Gridiron (blocking and tackling) Weightlifting Rugby league and rugby union (backs)
7	Excited	Running (200 and 400 metres) Swimming races Wrestling and judo Running very long and very short races

Continued

		Shotput and running long jump
		Rugby league and rugby union (halfback)
		Rowing
6	Moderate arousal	Boxing
		Basketball skills
		Gymnastic skills
		Soccer
		High jumping
5		Baseball pitchers and batters
		Gridiron quarterback
		Fencing
		Tennis and table tennis
		Cricket batting and bowling
		Golf (woods and long irons)
4	Slight arousal	Archery
		Bowling
		Ball catching
		Set place goal kicks (all football codes)
		Golf putting and short irons
		Basketball free throws
3	Normal waking state	
2	Deep relaxation	
1	Sleep	
0	You are now dead	

Adapted from: J.B. Oxendine (1970), 'Emotional Arousal and Motor Performance', *Quest*, 13:23-30.

Not only can these key words and colours be used before a contest, they can also be used during the actual competition to overcome any distractions or 'loss of concentration'. Take a pause or call time-out, take the time to repeat the words to yourself, think of your colour and then focus all your physical, psychological and intellectual energies — all in fine harmony — on the task at hand.

As we said at the beginning of this chapter there is a measure of aggression in every sport. Successful competition demands that this aggression be controlled through the careful manipulation of the arousal level. However, in any sporting contest the nature of the task (such as dribbling or free-throwing in basketball) and the current situation (for example, the score), combine to place fluctuating demands on the arousal level. Your intelligent manipulation of your own arousal level is dependent on an intelligent analysis of your game and skills, plus willingness to experiment until you develop the ritual which strikes the balance between arousal and performance which your sport demands.

7
THE ROLE OF IMAGINATION

Imagination, that essential component of our dreams and fantasies, is one of the most powerful influences in our lives. Consider the reaction of a normal person who is shown a 30 centimetre wide plank lying on the ground and asked to walk along it. Now anyone could accomplish that task with ease—they could walk, run, skip, somersault or even walk along it on their hands. But lift that plank eight stories high and suspend it between two steel girders and set that same person the same task. In nearly every case the person is paralysed by fear. A task which should be easily achieved is thwarted by the influence of imagination. And this brings us to a much ignored fact of life, a fact really only exploited in hypnosis, and that is that imagination *always* dominates the will.

One other aspect of imagination which is not so obvious is that in our imaginings of the real world, 'I' also intrudes and is of fundamental importance. However, because the presence of 'I' is so common we tent to ignore our mind's picture of 'I' and although 'I' is extremely retiring from a very early age we have a picture in our mind's eye of what we look like. Although this picture may be imperfect in the sense that it does not match either photographs or mirror images, it can be transposed onto paper. This is our self-image.

Now just as our imaginings about the real world can have a powerful immediate influence on our actions so too, our self-image can influence our lives. However the influence of self-image is more subtle and long term and it is increasingly recognized that the picture we construct of 'I', whether smiling, gloomy, confident or depressed, is an accurate reflection of how we make our way in this world.

In other words we become what we think we are. A nice

working concept, but so difficult to prove. The subjective experience tells us that it is true — but that is the core of the experience. Subjective. And, like fingerprints, no two people ever hold identical sets of beliefs about themselves and it is thus very difficult to get a measure of the individual's concept of himself or manipulate that self-image for experimental purposes. However, in the case of someone who is hypnotized and told that he is a lamp-post, then to all intents and purposes he sees himself as, and 'behaves' like, a lamp-post. If he is told that a plank on the ground is, in reality, eight stories up and there is the possibility that he may fall, then his imagination will prescribe the fear which will prevent him from walking across. If he is led to believe or imagine that vinegar is champagne, he will drink it with the same gusto normally associated with champagne.

To jump back to normal life, if we lack confidence in our abilities — if, for example, we imagine we are hopeless ball-catchers or plankwalkers — then we will never be able to catch a ball or walk the plank until we change our perception of ourselves and our abilities.

To the hypnotherapist, self-image is a working concept. A tool to be used in therapy. Manipulation and the creation of new images, and then feeding these images into the susceptible psyche of the patient, is the very crux of hypnotherapy. However, some hypnotherapists often unquestioningly accept that certain desired phenomena can be induced in the course of therapy without a full understanding of the reasons behind them. This situation arises through a lack of time combined with a poor academic background.

In contrast, research psychologists, with the time and inclination to explore the ramifications of the concept of self-image, approach it in the most cautious fashion. After all it is a big concept, encapsulating a host of delicate imponderables which are extremely difficult to quantify. No-one can really know and measure what another person thinks, and this difficulty is neatly matched by the problem of following the future course of that person and seeing and measuring whether imagination has been translated into reality.

The individual can have no objective appreciation of his self-image. He wanders through life a victim of apparently directionless fantasies mixed with the external reality.

Sometimes things are good; sometimes he is literally crushed by the burden of living. The only glimpse that the individual may ever catch of the workings of self-image is on those odd occasions when things are going well and he is buoyant and confident—then the external reality gets better and better and he seems incapable of doing any wrong. Conversely, when things are going badly and he expects the worst, then he gets the worst. To these individuals that is just one other facet of the burden of reality.

And here we have the common problem of the dichotomy between the subjective and the objective. People either subjectively know or make use of the concept of self-image or study it in an uncertain fashion. But make no mistake about it, self-image is one of the most important concepts psychology has unearthed in this century and, although quantification or objective knowledge is restricted, we believe that there are enough diverse sprinkles of information and observation to jump beyond the equivocation of the hard-minded researchers into a very basic appreciation of the concept of self-image and the crucial role it plays in directing our lives. We have compiled this series of observations and experiments, sometimes using hypnosis, which, taken as a whole, emphasize this role. We begin with the more general phenomena of phantom limbs and progress to the more specific.

The Phantom Limb Phenomenon

If we return to the picture we can draw of ourselves, we find that two parts of the picture which we usually have no trouble in drawing are the arms and legs. They have always been and will always remain a part of us. But what happens when we lose an arm or leg through accident or illness?

The immediate and often horrifying sensation is that the limb is still there. The amputee can still feel the wriggling of fingers or toes, feel the sensations of heat and cold and the texture of the bedclothes against the limb and is still aware of the unmistakable aura of pain associated with the original injury to the limb. This is the phantom limb phenomenon and the classic example of the perceived reality of the phantom limb is the oft-repeated case of the bedazed patient waking in the middle of the night and attempting to walk to the toilet on a non-existent leg.

Virtually every amputee suffers from phantom limbs and there are several aspects of the phenomenon relevant to our interest in self-image. First, the perception of the phantom limb in adults generally diminishes slowly, although in many cases the phantom limb remains a permanent fixture. In contrast, the phantom limb of child amputees disappears relatively quickly. It would appear that with children, where the role of the affected limb has not been permanently etched into the subconscious, they can suffer the loss of the limb with less psychic trauma than the adult who has a relatively inflexible view of his body. This interpretation is supported by the observation that children born with a congentially absent or truncated limb never experience the phantom, because they have never had the opportunity to formulate the image.

Mental Practice

A number of studies have shown that a mental rehearsal of an upcoming performance (or 'skull practice', in football parlance) can improve the result in the eventual performance. In one experiment, Dr R. Vandell, a psychologist, showed that mental practice in dart throwing — where the subject sits in front of the target and only imagines throwing darts at the board — improves dart throwing skills to the same level as if the subject has spent the time actually throwing darts.

In a similar study on the effects of mental practice on basketball free-throws, three groups of randomly selected students were scored on their basket-throwing ability and then, over the next twenty days, were subjected to the following routine:

One group engaged in no practice whatsoever in those twenty days.

The second group practised free-throws for twenty minutes every day.

The third group spent twenty minutes each day simply imagining that they were throwing the ball at the basket.

After those twenty days the first group, as could be expected, showed no improvement in their ability. The second group, through the agency of daily practice, improved their scoring rate by 24 per cent. The third group whose practice had been confined to the skull, improved their scoring ability by the similar margin of 23 per cent.

In both the above studies the subjects had a clear idea of what they wanted to achieve and simply imagined themselves mobilizing their bodies in the direction of that goal. It didn't really matter if their style was awkward. The subjects had marked out a goal and marked out the pathway which their body would follow to reach that goal, and the body followed the mind.

A related view on the importance of mental practice in sport was presented some twenty years ago by Johnny Bulla, a prominent professional golfer, who argued that having a clear mental image of where you wanted the ball to go is more important than 'form'. According to Bulla, most professional golfers have at least one serious flaw in their style yet still manage to play good golf. The reason, said Bulla, is that even though their stance or grip may be wrong, their goal-seeking subconscious mind takes over and directs the muscles to do whatever is necessary to compensate for the 'poor' style.

Another pro' golfer, Ben Hogan, mentally rehearses every shot he plays — 'feeling' the clubhead striking the ball and 'feeling' the perfect follow-through. Hogan relies on this mental practice to develop a 'muscle memory' that can be translated into a 'form' shot.

There are numerous other examples concerning the benefits of mental rehearsal in fields as diverse as salesmanship and music, but one neglected example, which we think is worth noting, is the use of 'special' exercises prescribed by coaches for athletes with 'special' problems. These exercises can be related to any of the numerous problems which afflict athletes whether it be poor grip, footwork, lazy knees or a crooked neck during a running race. Often these exercises are so weird and wonderful that they defy any objective justification.

Our assertion is that any improvement in the athlete's style or performance can be attributed to the mental concentration on the problem rather than to any changes in body musculature or functioning. In other words, at regular intevals the athlete is forced, by the very nature of the exercise, to think about the problem at hand and, since the coach has probably demonstrated the solution, that athlete has a clear picture of what he is trying to achieve and practises it mentally with every execution of the 'special' exercise. Any benefits which flow from that special exercise are due to the mental, not the physical, nature of the exercise.

School Achievement

Probably the most valuable quantification of the concept of self-image comes from educationists' studies of attitudes and performance of students. Numerous studies have demonstrated that students who expect to do well perform to their expectations. Again: we become what we think we are.

We will only mention one important study, the so-called Brookover study, conducted in the United States over a six-year period between 1962 and 1968. This study related the self-concept of academic ability to school achievement amongst students in one class followed from the seventh through to the twelfth grade.

Amongst the findings were that the reported self-concept (self-assessment) of ability was significantly related to achievement and that this relationship persisted even when the effects of differing intelligence were taken into account. Another point worth noting is that a student's achievements at school seemed to be limited only by the student's own concept of his or her abilities.

Through a synthesis of a number of studies a composite portrait of the successful student would produce the picture of an adolescent who has a relatively high opinion of himself and is optimistic about his future performance. He also has confidence in his ability in other activities beside school-work and needs fewer favourable evaluations from others to spur him on to achievement. He also feels that he works hard and is liked and accepted by other students.

In contrast, and to a certain extent, predictably, under-achieving students are, amongst other things, self-derogatory and have a depressed attitude towards themselves, with feelings of inadequacy and inferiority. Their low and derogatory self-image seems to dictate that they perform at a low level.

Another point worth noting is that even when performance exceeds expectations the student with a low self-image will be unhappy about the event and tend to make excuses for the performance. Several studies have shown that students who perform poorly but expected to do so, were more satisfied than those who had performed well but had not expected or anticipated this turn of events. These 'good' performers experienced considerable discomfort and tended to assess their performance in terms which reduced it to the level of their expectations.

These studies show that the self-image is ultra-conservative and that individuals are generally unwilling to accept evidence that is contrary to the way they perceive themselves. They always resolve conflict between evidence and personal judgement in favour of personal judgement. The amputee who unconsciously attempts to walk on a non-existent leg is opting for personal judgement. In the same fashion, if an individual wrongly considers himself to be a particularly stylish tennis player and this perception is important to that individual's concept of himself and his social standing, then it will take many failures and great patience on the part of his coach to convince him otherwise.

Our self-image is always striving for consistency and resists change to an amazing degree. This is what is known as being set in our ways. But why do we do it?

Far from being negative, resistance to change of our self-image is a positive feature of our lives: if our perceived self or self-image was continually fluctuating through a wide gamut of laudatory and derogatory perceptions, then we would never know where we stood in this world. We would lack a consistent personality and our loved ones, assuming they remained unchanged, could probably not tolerate us. For every one of us, no matter how negative our self-image may be, the crucial issues of *who* and *what 'I' am* are essential to our existence. Almost anything is better than no self-image, because if we ever reach the state of having no self-image then we become truly *nothing*.

Hypnotic Contraception and Breast Enlargement

After the heading above you may well be pondering the leap from learned discussion on amputation, skull practice and school to the sudden mysteries of birth control and breast enhancement. However, stay with us. Although the phenomena would appear to be just two more of the weird and wonderful aspects of hypnosis, they provide fascinating examples of the malleability of the self-image and the control of bodily functions — even when these functions relate to apparently automatic and permanent physical fixtures such as ovulation and breast size. We will first discuss the phenomenon of breast enlargement.

Psychological problems associated with small breasts are just one of the many problems that confront the clinical hypnotist and, surprisingly, it is also a problem that is amenable to hypnotherapy. From clinical experience it appears that nearly every woman has a certain amount of 'slack' which can be taken up through hypnosis and bust increases of 2.5 to 5 centimetres are regularly achieved. Although this would appear to be an almost insignificant increase, the psychological effects are profoundly rewarding.

How does the hypnotherapist help mould a new shape for a woman? Here, once again, we return to the power of imagination. The subject is hypnotized and trained to practice self-hypnosis with the aid of a tape-recording. The focus of the hypnotic suggestion is, of course, on the breasts. The subject is encouraged to see herself as she would like to be and, at the same time, to experience feelings of heaviness and warmth in the breasts. The body reacts to these suggestions and over a one to three month period the breasts slowly enlarge.

There has been little scientific interest in this phenomenon but one small study is worth recounting. This study is unique in the sense that it rejected the tape measure as the arbiter of breast dimensions. The tape measure is inaccurate because it is measuring many other parts of the body besides the breasts — most importantly, the muscles of the back and shoulders which through tension and flexing can distort the bust measure. As an alternative, Dr Roy Beran, a neurologist at the Adelaide Children's Hospital, with an active interest in hypnosis, used as a measure the volume of water displaced by each breast when it is immersed in a bowl.

Reporting his initial results to the National Convention of Hypnotherapists, held in Adelaide in February 1979, Beran demonstrated that breast volume could be increased substantially through hypnosis. The subject, a woman with small and uneven breasts — the left breast displaced 120 cubic centimetres (cc) of water while the right breast displaced only 66 cc — increased the breast volume over a three month period to 260 cc for the left and 290 cc for the right breast.

The hormonal and other physiological changes associated with this increase are unknown. All we can say with any certainty is that the woman saw how she wanted to be, felt how she wanted to be, and the influence of her subconscious mind was powerful enough to direct her bodily functions in that direction.

In the case of hypnotic contraception we are dealing with two different approaches to a problem. Firstly, hypnosis has been used with women athletes who have the complication of a menstrual period due at the same time as an important competition. Here hypnotic suggestion is used to either advance or delay menstruation. With hypnotic contraception we are really referring to hypnotically induced abortion. However, the principles behind both are similar; we will deal with the abortion phenomenon.

Among women there is a condition known as hysterical sterility where, for no apparent reason, a fertile woman is incapable of conceiving. The reason for the sterility is to be found in the anxiety and apprehension the woman feels about child-bearing and rearing. In most cases the sterility is dramatically reversed after the adoption of a child, when most of the anxiety concerning children is dispelled.

What is notable in this condition is that a 'state of mind' is involved and that this 'state of mind' can inhibit conception. In a way still not understood, hypnotic suggestion can be used to recreate this state of mind without inducing any of the associated anxiety.

The suggestions which are offered have the effect of guiding the woman into feeling that she is in control of her reproductive system and, given her present position, where it is inadvisable for her to conceive (for whatever reason), she can transform her womb in such a way that it is hostile to the fertilized ovum. It is suggested that in the future she will only be able to conceive when she has made a conscious decision to do so after having regard for all the circumstances at the time.

In a review of 28 cases of hypnotic abortion by Brian Perry, an Adelaide hypnotherapist, it was shown that 26 of these women either aborted within 48 hours or the fertilized ovum was reabsorbed and the woman resumed menstruation on or about the usual time. Again the subconscious mind coupled to the power of imagination appears to be able to direct the body along a desired and imagined path.

Facial Muscle Activity

When we smile or look gloomy or contemplate any of the other emotions the face is capable of expressing, the four major muscle groups of the face — the frontalis, corrugator, masseter and depressor — combine to produce the appropriate look.

Even very low levels of emotion can still affect the muscles—some will tense and some will relax. Yet these subliminal movements will not be noticeable to either a casual observer or the person concerned.

In a series of studies led by Professor Gary Schwartz, a psychologist at Harvard University, a number of subjects were hooked-up to electrodes capable of detecting subtle changes in facial muscle activity. The subjects were told to lie back and relax and then requested to generate happy, sad or angry imagery.

Although there was no change in facial expression, movements in the muscle recordings showed that just thinking a happy, sad or angry thought produced the muscle response typical of that emotion. When these normal subjects were asked to think about a 'typical day' they generated a muscle pattern very similar to the happiness pattern.

Schwartz and his co-workers then turned their attention to a group of clinically depressed people. When tested in the same way as the group of normal subjects, the depressives produced muscle patterns comparable to those of normal subjects for sadness and anger. However, they could. not produce the muscle response typical of happiness. When asked to think of a typical day the resulting muscle activity was one of sadness.

As Schwartz commented in one of his publications: 'The ability of affective imagery to produce discrete muscular patterns supports the view that specific self-induced cognitive states can generate discrete bodily patterns'. In other words, when we think happy, sad or angry thoughts the body unconsciously follows those thoughts. We become what we think we are.

Psychosomatic Disease

The number of illnesses known to be products of the mind is quite large. At the last count some 150 afflictions, ranging from skin disorders such as eczema and psoriasis, through to digestive complaints and more serious conditions such as hysterical blindness and deafness, are considered to be of psychosomatic origin. The list is quite extensive and still growing as we slowly become aware of the psychological input in human illness.

Consider the various diseases of the heart. These do have an organic origin but researchers have shown that certain personality types are most susceptible to heart disease. In these cases the distictive personality of the victim dictates that he follow a heart-damaging lifestyle. However, this is not all there is to death from heart disease.

In a survey conducted by Dr A. Appels and his colleagues in Holland, it was shown that those individuals who have developed what Appels classes the 'giving-up syndrome' have a much higher than normal chance of experiencing a heart attack in the future. These people answer 'yes' to such leading questions as: 'Do you sometimes feel that your body is a battery losing power?' or 'Do you find it harder to endure loud noises?' or 'Do you sometimes feel the urge to quit?' Such people see themselves as running out of steam and life and they have, literally, given up the ghost. How many similar examples will be found if some one takes the time to look?

A particular study, which we think is one of the most provocative and illuminating pieces of research into the nature of personality and psychosomatic disease — a truly 'sick' variant of the self-image concept — was presented in a series of experiments conducted by Professor David Graham a psychiatrist from the University of Wisconsin. Along with his co-workers, he defined the attitudes of people afflicted with a range of psychosomatic conditions and then, using hypnosis as an experimental tool, suggested these attitudes to perfectly normal people and then measured the response. These studies were published in *Psychosomatic Medicine* and the *Journal of Psychosomatic Research.*

Graham taped detailed interviews with 128 people who were variously afflicted with eleven psychosomatic conditions. The questions revolved around these individuals' attitudes to living and attempted to probe the events which either precipitated or exacerbated their condition. The tapes of these interviews were carefully edited to remove any reference to the patient's illness and then played back to a panel of four judges who were asked to define the attitude of each patient.

Three psychosomatic disorders and their associated disorders were selected for further study. The selection being based on the ease of measuring the physiological changes associated with each disorder.

Hives (Urticaria), is a common skin complaint which consists of transitory swellings, known as weals, which vary from about one centimetre across to covering very large areas. The condition may last for hours or, in extreme cases, persist for years. Hives is associated with warmth or an increase in skin temperature. The panel defined the attitude of the hives sufferer as being one where the individual felt he was taking a beating and was helpless to do anything about it.

Raynaud's disease, causes the flow of blood to the extremities, the fingers and toes, to be restricted. Less commonly, the nose, cheeks and ears have their bloodflow restricted. The direct cause is to be found in a spasm in the arterioles, the small blood vessels which connect the arteries to the capillaries. This spasm blocks the flow of blood and results in the affected part of the body taking on a blanched or waxen colour and becoming cold; when cut, there is very little blood associated with the wound. If the condition persists the area may take on a grey colour and feelings of numbness, tingling and sometimes pain are associated with the disorder. In extreme cases gangrene may set in. As could be expected, a drop in skin temperature, due to the lack of warming blood, is characteristic of the disease. The panel described the mental attitude associated with Raynaud's disease as a very basic desire to commit a hostile and aggressive act.

Essential hypertension, or high blood pressure, is a common cause of death in modern man. Evidence is accumulating that the stresses and strains of modern life are associated with the complaint. There are usually three mechanisms of death from high blood pressure: heart failure, cerebral haemorrhage or kidney failure. As could be expected, the physiological measure of essential hypertension is easily measured. And the attitude? Not surprisingly it relates back to stress; according to the panel the individual suffering from high blood pressure always feels threatened and experiences the need to be ready for anything in order to cope with the imminent, harmful event.

The discovery of specific attitudes associated with psychosomatic conditions was an important finding in itself but, Graham wondered, what would happen if otherwise normal people adopted some of these attitudes? Would their temperatures fluctuate in tune with the attitudes? Was it possible to increase blood pressure by the adoption of the hypertensive attitude? And, at this stage, hypnosis was used as the tool to introduce these attitudes into the psyche of a perfectly normal subject.

Seated comfortably and hooked up to instruments which were measuring skin temperature and blood pressure, a carefully-screened selection of university and theological students were tested under controlled conditions. During the two-hour session the subject, after temperature and blood pressure had stabilized, was hypnotized and then told to relax while temperature and blood pressure were recorded during a ten-minute control period. The subject was then given an attitude suggestion for ten minutes and asked to relax again for a further ten minutes. A different attitude was then suggested for the next ten minutes, followed by another period of relaxation, and so on, until the end of the session.

The attitudes that were suggested related back to the attitudes of sufferers of the disease as defined by the panel in Graham's earlier study. The suggestions ran as follows.

For Hives the subject was touched on the hand with an unlit match and told that 'Dr X is now going to burn your hand with a match. When he does so you will feel very much mistreated, very unfairly treated, but you will be unable to do anything about it. You can't even think of anything you want to do about it, you just have to take it. You are thinking only of what has happened to you.'

For the Raynaud's disease attitude the procedure was the same except that the subject was told that: 'You feel mistreated and you want to hit Dr X. You want to hit him and choke him and strangle him. That's all you're thinking about, how much you want to hit him.'

The hypertension suggestion ran as follows: 'Dr X is going to burn you or shock you or do something else to you that may be painful. It may injure you, it may even be dangerous. You have to be ready for whatever he's going to do, you have to be alert and on guard and try to be prepared. You just have to wait for something that may be painful or dangerous. You can't prevent it. You feel you are in danger and you have to watch out, to be ready for anything.'

The results of the study confirmed Graham's predictions. When the subject had the hypertension suggestion put to him, his blood pressure increased; when the hives suggestion was offered, his skin temperature increased; and when the attitude associated with Raynaud's disease was fed into the system, the skin temperature dropped.

Now it is a common hypnotic phenomenon that a subject can manipulate the temperature of hands or feet through the agency of suggestions relating to warmth and blood circulation. However, in Graham's studies no such direct suggestion was involved, only indirect suggestions, relating to a state of mind, were used to manipulate bodily functions. Once again, the adoption of a particular state of mind dictated that the body react to and follow the pathway that flowed from that state of mind. In this case the mind adopts a psychosomatic attitude and the body follows by adopting a psychosomatic reaction.

If we turn Graham's findings upside down and consider them from the point of view of a normal person then it appears obvious that the normal person should be able, by adopting specific mental attitudes, to influence the functions of his body. We refer specifically to the control of blood pressure which, as we pointed out in our earlier chapter, is an important component in the arousal process.

To illustrate the nature of this control we will now describe some experiments in biofeedback also conducted by Professor Gary Schwartz. Biofeedback is a big field, and we will not pursue the subject too far. Biofeedback studies involve the subject being given constant information on internal responses such as brain wave activity, heart rate and blood pressure plus incentives or rewards for changing those internal responses. They have shown that people can control a wide range of their muscles and functions which, before the 1960s, were thought to be incapable of conscious control. For many of these biofeedback exercises only a few sessions are necessary before the subject can control the function under study almost at will.

Professor Schwartz was interested in the control of heart rate. He showed that a group of subjects who were instructed to 'control and raise your heart rate' when one light came on, and to 'control and lower your heart rate' when another light flashed on, could easily manipulate their heart rate, with a variation of around eight pulses per minute. The important point is that when those subjects were asked what thoughts they used to generate the changes in the heart rate, they reported that they thought of angry, aggressive, tense or sexual images while raising the heart rate and had quiet, relaxing fantasies while lowering the heart rate.

Adopting a different tack, Schwartz changed the instruction to 'think arousing thoughts' without any mention of controlling the heart rate. The result was that, despite the arousing thoughts of anger, tension and sex, the heart rate did not increase by any significant measure. According to Schwartz the subjects seemed to expend so much attention and energy on the generation of arousing thoughts that there was a relative inhibition of body movement and the heart rate would not increase. As Schwartz commented: 'Apparently there is a major difference between *having* a fantasy and *acting* upon it'. The lesson here is that if we want to arouse ourselves, if we want to use mental imagery to manipulate our body functions, then we need to direct that imagery at a goal — whether the goal is increasing the heart rate or improving a sporting performance. Imagery and goals — that is the essence of control.

If there is one outstanding lesson to be learnt from this book, it relates to defining appropriate goals. We accept that no one can be instantly transformed from B-grade to world championship status. But anyone can make the best of their abilities by setting goals, defining a fresh self in terms of those goals and then working towards those goals. If they make world championship status in the process, then that is only an incidental benefit associated with their new definition of self because, as we have shown above, the importance and the degree of control achievable through the manipulation of self is apparently enormous.

If we lose a leg we still 'feel' it; if we rehearse our actions in a relaxed, non-commital fashion, then our final actions will conform to that rehearsal; if we think we are 'good' students then we become 'good' students; if we think happy thoughts our facial muscles automatically and unconsciously respond; if we are trapped in a peculiar psychological warp we can become ill; if we want to work at it we can manipulate our heart rate, blood pressure, breast size or reproductive activities.

If we imagine ourselves to be champions, if we set ourselves a progression of realistic goals and are prepared to devote time and energy to the pursuit of that image, then there will come a time when we reach that highest goal. The only limits to our abilities are those we impose upon ourselves and a positive self-image knows no bounds. Keep this in mind.

8
PHYSICAL PERFORMANCE AFTER HYPNOSIS

We have referred to the potential strength of the human body, but just how far can muscle be pushed? How strong is muscle? The plain answer is *very strong*. Muscle is stronger than bone and bone will always break before the muscle that moves it. In the early years of electroconvulsive therapy (ECT), patients regularly broke bones in the throes of their convulsions and this problem was only solved by the introduction of muscle relaxants.

Muscle contracts, or works, after receiving an electrical stimulus via the nerves and, it is worth stating the obvious, the will to move that muscle always precedes the nervous impulse and the eventual contraction of the muscle. As work continues, the muscle requires a larger electrical stimulus to activate its contraction and, at the same time, begins to consume more oxygen than the blood vessels can supply. To overcome this oxygen deficit, the muscle cells switch over to an anaerobic process (that is, without oxygen) to fuel the biochemical cycles which provide the energy to move the muscle. A by-product of this anaerobic process is lactic acid which in high concentrations is toxic.

Oxygen starvation and lactic acid build-up are responsible for the pain of fatigue; but the muscle is still capable of contraction for a long time after the first twinges of pain are felt. All that is needed is a continuation of those nervous impulses which began that muscle's movement. However, it is a fact of life that most people stop working after enduring only a small amount of pain. The will always breaks before the muscle; this is one of the truisms of work. In other words the decision processes in the brain, regulating the contraction of that muscle, always tire before that muscle's energy reserves are exhausted.

There is another truism, straight from the hypnotist's experience, which is worth introducing here and that is: the imagination *always* triumphs over the will. In other words the conscious mind may, in its logical fashion, tell a man who is running and performing an endurance test on a treadmill, that he is tired and should stop. If that man's imagination is influenced, however, by a hypnotic suggestion to the effect that he is being chased by murderous savages, then his imagination, providing the suggestion hits home, will dominate his will to quit. That man will find miraculous reserves of energy, burst through one of those metaphorical pain barriers, and keep running.

The question of whether hypnosis can improve physical performance has interested psychologists and physiologists for some time. It is an intriguing question because to all outward appearances it is a question that should be resolved by numbers: numbers expressing performance before and after hypnosis. In contrast, the benefits of hypnosis in team or one-to-one contests can only be assessed subjectively — scores or numbers are virtually meaningless. A host of explanations are trotted out every time a team or individual, using hypnosis, turns the tide in their match performances. The losing team or individual may have had an 'off' day, or suffered from a hostile referee, or could have been unlucky or complacent. But sheer numbers should convince any cynic.

Numbers involve addition, subtraction, division, multiplication, and averaging. In other words: statistics. And to arrive at the correct statistical answer any experimenter must face up to the incredible rigmarole which is the scientific method. In fact the method is more important than the numbers. Let us put that question of methodology to one side for just one moment, and ask that very basic question: what are the numbers like?

We will be perfectly honest: fickle. Numbers are fraught with experimental problems and error, open to the twin questions of differing arousal levels and suggestion. The results are dependent on the skill of the hypnotist, the whims and statistical vagaries of measurement and the individual subject's inherent variability. However, if we pick our way carefully through this maze of complications it is clear that a trend, culminating in more recent studies, confirms that hypnosis can improve any individual's physical performance. Let us look back to some of the more recent studies and some of the problems involved in those studies.

As we have emphasized throughout, the most crucial input in hypnosis is the quality of the suggestion and, in the area of straight physical performance, the most crucial input is a high arousal level. Depth of trance is relatively unimportant.

In the case of scientists' studying the effects of hypnosis on physical performance, there is a great demand for standardization of the experimental technique. This arises through that very basic dogma which demands that every experiment should be repeatable. As a result, the scientist always chooses to work with subjects who are in the 'deepest' possible trance — since specifying 'deepest' cuts out any possible equivocation. In the same way, suggestion is standardized. The only variant is the name of the subject. Surprisingly, no monitoring of arousal levels has been attempted. Combine these basic deficiencies with the statistical limitations imposed by working with small groups of people and you have some insight into the equivocation which occurs when the topic of hypnosis and muscular performance and endurance is raised.

Possibly, experimental groups of 400 individuals randomly assigned to four groups of 100 and subject to the scientific method, could tolerate a standard pattern of suggestion and produce a statistically significant result. But what experimenter is capable of organizing, testing and analysing such a large group? The realities of the experimental life dictate that small groups — usually of less than twenty — are the subjects in the experiment. And these are the people who receive the standardized suggestion.

Any working hypnotherapist would scoff at the thought of using a standard line of suggestion when attempting to take different patients to a similar end. Every individual has unique needs and susceptibilities which a skilful hypnotist, un-encumbered by the demands of the scientific method, expects to exploit. Thus, in the case of arousing a football team, a competent hypnotist will note such indicators of arousal as fist-clenching and teeth-gritting or, more commonly, an increase in the respiration rate, to see whether his subjects are getting the message. If a response is not evident he can change his tack, introducing a new line or pattern of suggestion which, hopefully, will produce the arousal response which is so crucial to the maximum performance demanded. For the working hypnotherapist who expects to get results, who is paid on the basis of those results, there can be no such thing as a standard suggestion.

We begin our survey of the literature on hypnosis and performance in the late 1950s with a series of studies conducted by Professor Warren Johnson and co-workers from the University of Maryland. Johnson, writing in *Research Quarterly* summarized earlier studies, going back to the 1930s, in the following words: 'Most experimental reports of motor performance are favourable to hypnotic and post-hypnotic suggestion. In some instances, the advantage of hypnotic and/or post-hypnotic performance was found to be highly significant statistically.' We choose Johnson's work as a starting point because of the rigorous nature of his studies and the fact that he used athletes, in good physical condition. Here he was looking for those few percentage points on top of the normal performance to prove the efficacy of hypnosis. In contrast, the earlier studies referred to by Johnson used non-athletes, and the greater room for improvement was probably reflected in their favourable assessment of hypnosis.

In one of Johnson's studies, ten athletes and/or physical education students were hypnotized and then tested on a bicycle ergometer (to measure work output) for an 'all-out effort' over one hundred revolutions. The tests compared performance while hypnotized against performance while hypnotized plus acting under the influence of a suggestion delivered in a 'deliberate, quiet but authoritative manner'. The suggestion was to the effect that 'The subject's legs would feel and be especially strong, his endurance would be especially good, fatigue would not set in as soon as usual or be as severe or painful, and he would make an extraordinarily good ride. He was also told that he would recover quickly and feel good after the ride.' The subjects were also given suggestions for post-hypnotic amnesia so they would not know whether they had received the bracket of performance suggestions or recall any details of the tests.

The results showed only a slight improvement in the time taken to complete 100 revolutions on the bicycle after receiving the performance suggestions. This improvement was not statistically significant, but the subjective reports of the subjects regarding their condition after the tests were consistently better after suggestion was used. In other words, the subjects responded to the hypnotic suggestions by feeling less fatigued and recovering more rapidly after their 'all-out' effort.

In the above study, the suggestions used were of a very low-key nature and, in an attempt to define the importance of suggestion, Johnson and his co-workers assembled another group of ten athletes and then tested their ability to bench press, to exhaustion, a 47 pound (21.4 kilogram) barbell, while under the influence of a range of suggestions. These ranged from a stereotyped suggestion pattern which was concerned with 'developing a state of mind' to perform well. A pep-talk suggestion, which attempted to stir up the subjects by appealing to their egos, was given in 'an urgent, rather excited but not loud or hysterical manner'. The third suggestion was post-hypnotic, a suggestion which would become operative after the hypnotic session, when the experimenter would make a signal during the test, which would have an invigorating, refreshing effect on the subject. The fourth suggestion was a failure suggestion, made as a quiet statement of fact, that the subjects could not possibly do as well as usual because, whether by mistake or design, they would think that extra weight had been added to the barbell and their fatigue would be much greater than usual. It should be noted that every test involved hypnosis and no test was made of the subjects' abilities while in their normal state.

When the subjects were tested the 'pep-talk' suggestion was slightly, but not statistically better than the other positive suggestions. The failure suggestions always provoked a statistically significant decline in performance. Some of the subjects who could press the weight some fifty times under the influence of a positive suggestion would struggle to reach thirty when hindered by suggestions of failure. As Johnson commented: 'As the subjects began to tire sooner than usual, they would glance anxiously at the barbell weights, try desperately to continue, and when they finished they expressed wonder at, and/or apologised for, their poor performance'.

The effectiveness of the failure-type suggestion confirms earlier studies. Indeed, if there is one rule about hypnosis and performance it is that negative suggestions are always effective.

No matter if they are athletes who are trained to resist fatigue or the proverbial 'man off the street' — if they are led to believe that they will fail, then they fail — and to a statistically significant degree. There are obvious implications for every sportsman in this fact.

Apart from the effectiveness of negative suggestions, the problems of statistics, especially when a few percentage points of improvement are involved, intrude into any study on hypnosis and performance. Statistics is a science which attempts to even out the bumps and quantify some measure of a sample (of a population) and then tries to assess whether that measure means that one population is different from another. Every statistican has difficulties with a sample involving only ten measures, unless the differences are clear-cut. Yet there are times when extreme differences in measurement provide just as many problems. Such a problem confronted Johnson in the third study which involved, besides the bench press, tests for hand grip strength and the ability to jump and reach.

Starting again with ten subjects and using stereotyped suggestions, Johnson found that he had to exclude one subject from the statistical analysis because of his phenomenal performance in the bench press. Even though this aberrant individual was excluded, the data from the other subjects showed a statistically significant increase in their ability to perform the bench press while under the influence of hypnotic suggestion. Other tests showed slight (1-1.5 per cent) increases in performance under hypnosis but these differences were not statistically significant.

Our concern is the subject who had to be excluded from the bench press results. There is a lesson here.

This particular subject was a professional athlete and habitual weight trainer who, in a series of four pre-study practice sessions, was able to press the 47 pound barbell approximately 130 times; much more than any of the other subjects. While these other subjects showed a significant, though marginal, improvement in their bench-pressing ability, this subject went into the test sessions and performed his usual 130 presses when suggestions only were offered. But once hyonosis *and* suggestions were combined he pressed 180 (when he was stopped by a worried experimenter) and then, under the influence of a new pattern of suggestion, 230 (when he was stopped again) and 333 when he was allowed to press on until exhaustion. At this stage, when everyone else was pressing in the 40 to 50 range, he was excluded from the study because of his perplexing performance. In hindsight, what can we make of such a number?

In any population, whether it be a nation state or an experimental group, there is a tremendous variation in ability. Johnson's group of ten subjects had hit upon an extreme. And some points about this extreme are worth noting.

First of all, in a later interview it became clear that this subject took the suggestions offered by Johnson on their face value. Tucked away midst a whole pattern of strength promoting suggestions was the statement: 'Begin to feel now as though the success of a whole team or *saving your own or someone else's life* depends on your performance in these tests. . .' The subject really believed his performance *was* a matter of life and death.

Every ninety presses he suffered a crisis and tended to shake and falter but then, suddenly and presumably when his imagination had once again achieved the upper hand, he pressed on with renewed vigour.

Here once again, the crucial impact of suggestion raises its head.

Then, during the last stages of testing, the subject developed a new concept of his ability and potential; we can do no better than quote from Johnson's paper in Research Quarterly:

'After (one of the tests), when he had conscious recall of the testing, he stated repeatedly that he was quite sure that he could do no more but to his surprise would see his arms rise with the weight. As a habitual weight trainer this did not seem natural to him, and he was very much alarmed and considered withdrawing from the study. When he returned (for the final test) he spoke of having a new idea of his performance potentialities and had no doubt of his ability to do still better than before, which he did. . . He was then asked to return and press the weight without suggestions of any kind. He was certain that he could now do better than ever before because, he repeated, he had a new idea of what he could do. In this post-research testing he was stopped by the investigator at 350 presses. . . He reported a complete absence of muscular stiffness on the days following all tests.'

The subject now knew that he could press the weight at least 350 times but the effects of this new self-image went way beyond the experiment when the subject subsequently achieved top standing within his football team. Rightly or wrongly, this subject believed his success was due to the new knowledge of his potential he had gained through participating in Johnson's study.

Even Johnson, within the dry restrictions imposed by the scientific paper, seemed confounded by his results and commented: 'The remarkable performance by the professional athlete in this test is the kind of thing that greatly complicates the examination of hypnotic phenomena and encourages the use of such terminology as "transcendence of normal waking capacity" by means of hypnosis. Cases of this kind would seem to require an explanation beyond what has so far been proposed.' Can we dare to suggest that the explanation of this 'transcendence' lies in the mundane fact that the subject and experimenter, through sheer chance, had hit upon a suggestion pattern compatible with high performance? Remember that this subject believed that his performance was a matter of life and death and, as we know, during such periods of stress the body is capable of superhuman performance. It is worth asking what would have been the statistical result if every other subject was led to believe that they were fighting for their lives?

Johnson also referred to the problems inherent in using only a small number of subjects and pointed to a study published in 1951 by Dr Elsie Roush who, working with twenty subjects, found significant improvements in arm strength, grip strength and endurance. Is it not possible that the fact that this was such a large group was instrumental in achieving a statistically significant result?

One final point which is worth stressing about Johnson's studies is that all of the earlier studies he mentioned involved non-athletes, and the majority showed improvements in performance after hypnosis. In contrast, Johnson used athletes, usually in training, and presumably, near a physical peak. He was attempting to lift this peak a little further through hypnosis. To be statistically significant this lift would have to be in the order of 5-10 per cent and be uniformly distributed. In only one of the five tests conducted by Johnson was such an improvement obvious. In the other four tests, however, hypnosis combined with suggestion (albeit standardized) produced a clearly improved performance. This improvement was as low as 0.6 per cent through to the statistically significant 5 per cent, but such small increments in performance are what separate champions from would-be champions.

From the time of Johnson's studies through to the 1970s, there was a dearth of studies into the question of hypnosis and performance. As can be concluded from the comments above, this situation most probably arose because of the daunting problems in methodology posed by such a personal topic as hypnotic suggestion and individual performance.

In an attempt to overcome these problems in methodology, some European scientists concentrated on the workings of the muscles involved in the test as well as measuring the endurance times. Any muscle will keep on contracting provided the electrical jolt provided by the nervous system is sufficiently large to jump into the action potential which causes the muscle to contract. With increasing work and fatigue this action potential rises. To follow the changes in action potential these scientists used a highly sensitive electromyogram to record the changes in muscle electrical activity.

However, before we continue it should be pointed out that in these two studies we come to another extreme in the problems of methodology which beset the studies on hypnosis and performance. In only one study (the Russian) was this detailed statistical analysis performed, and in both studies the comparison was simply between the unhypnotized and hypnotic state. The question of, and the importance of, suggestion does not come into the descriptions of either experimental method.

In the first study, conducted by scientists from the Soviet Research Institute of Work Hygiene and Occupational Diseases and published in the 1976 *Bulletin of Experimental Biology and Medicine,* subjects were tested for the ability of their arms to support a weight while the arm was in an outstretched and horizontal position. An experienced hypnotist assisted.

The results of the endurance test showed that, after hypnosis and some presumably 'rock-like' suggestions, the subjects were able to double the time that they could support the weight. On average this increase was from 66 to 133 seconds and was statistically significant.

Above: Russian physiologist, Ivan Pavlov, famed for his research on conditioned reflexes, who wrote of his work that 'hypnosis kept on obtruding into the foreground'.

Right: Franz Anton Mesmer, founder of mesmerism and, despite some flamboyant showmanship, a pioneer of modern hypnotherapy.

In 1976 Les Cunningham helped the Sydney University Boat Club. Their Junior Eight stunned officials by beating Senior and Junior crews to take the Riverview Gold Cup and the Australian Championship.

Alongside the increase in endurance times, the electrical activity in the muscles increased by 1.5 to 2 times. This result confirms the assertion that the will always breaks before the muscle. Any tiring muscle can be made to continue working so long as the will is prepared to direct an increasing electrical charge down the nerves to that muscle.

The second study, conducted by Finnish physiologists in 1977, also tested endurance but in this case it was the ability of a leg to maintain a push against a constant force; the electrical activity of the abdominal muscles involved in the push, was also monitored. Only three subjects were involved and no indication of the suggestions used in the tests was provided. In terms of results, this study contradicts the Russian study in the sense that no differences in muscle electrical activity, between the normal and hypnotic state, were observed. However, in terms of endurance the three subjects were able to maintain their push an extra 7,9 and 22 per cent longer (average 13 per cent) when performing under the influence of hypnosis combined with suggestion.

A different approach was adopted by two Australians, hypnotherapist, Dr Arthur Jackson and a physiologist, Dr Greg Gass. They used a range of physiological measures in their study of the effects of hypnosis and motivational suggestion on subjects' performances on a treadmill. In many respects this study is the most rigorous conducted to date, incorporating a large group (55) separation of low and highly hypnotizable subjects and a careful assessment of whether the individual was performing to his maximum ability. Against this, however, a standardized hypnotic routine and motivational suggestion was presented through the use of a tape recording.

Presenting their results at the Eighth International Congress of Hypnosis and Psychosomatic Medicine held in Melbourne in August 1979, Jackson and Gass concluded that 'subjects given motivational suggestions in the absence of hypnosis performed as well as the highly susceptible hypnotic group given identical motivational suggestions'. Although the differences between the two groups was not statistically significant, it should be pointed out that the treadmill endurance times increased by 8 per cent in the motivation group as against the 16 per cent in the hypnosis/motivation group.

We have presented a critique of the various experimental efforts relating hypnosis to performance and from our comments it is obvious that there are serious problems in the methodology of such studies. Some of these problems are:

1 How many subjects are needed to produce a statistically significant result?
2 Is the individual subject sufficiently motivated at the start of the experiment to perform at the best of his 'normal' ability?
3 How crucial is trance depth?
4 Where does the arousal level fit in?
5 How important is a relevant and meaningful suggestion pattern to the individual subject?

Accommodating these questions places impossible demands on experimental design and it is quite likely that the definitive experiment on hypnosis and muscular performance will never be performed because of these complications. In all likelihood we will have to be content with a continuing series of reports which are statistically and methodologically unsound, and which will only serve to tantalize us with their imperfect answer to the intriguing question of whether hypnosis can improve muscular performance. Despite this negative assessment, it is worth remembering that all the literature to date shows improvements in gross motor performance after hypnosis and suggestion. A continuation of such positive findings will eventually provide a neat sum which will confirm the ability of the will, influenced by hypnosis, to continue directing the muscles to perform long after they would normally stop.

9
MORE CASE STUDIES

Les Cunningham's casebook is crammed with examples of the successful use of hypnosis in sport. We can describe only a few of them in detail and we have been guided in our choice by the lessons to be learnt from those cases. Inevitably, this means that we have had to leave out many other fascinating instances of hypnosis in sport. They include cases such as the B-grade weightlifter who boosted his lifting power by 35 pounds (16 kilograms); the news editor of the *Dominion,* the New Zealand capital's largest newspaper, who, after hypnosis, defeated his long time rival and summed-up this victory in a brief note to Cunningham: 'Les, I thrashed the bastard at billiards today'; or the inexperienced university boxer whose ambition, coupled with the determination instilled by Cunningham, went on to thrash his way to the university championship. There are many such cases but we must confine ourselves to some of the more notable events:

The Australian skydiving team benefited from Cunningham's techniques when he used hypnotic suggestion to dispel fears and weld the individuals into a team which could function at 2.4 kilometres. This Australian team exceeded all expectations by finishing a close second in the 1975 World Championships in Germany.

Cunningham also hypnotized and primed New Zealand shot-putter, Bernie Harland, ('Just before you compete you will feel like a wound-up spring and then. . . Whack. . . you release the spring. . .') before he produced his best ever performance. Another New Zealander, tennis player Tony Parun, was hypnotized and inspired by Cunningham just before he beat the then Junior Wimbledon Champion, Chris Lewis, and then New Zealand's number one player Brian

Fairlie, in the final of a major New Zealand tournament in 1975. Parun later commented in a letter to Cunningham, that on the day he felt as though he could have beaten anyone in the world because every shot was going his way.

Paraplegic athletes have also benefited from Cunningham's involvement. In 1972 Cunningham assisted the paraplegic weightlifter, Vic Renalson, to beat his previous best effort and establish a new world record for the bench press, of 464 pounds (210.9 kilograms) — this lift was a new record for both paraplegic and 'normal' weightlifters. Another paraplegic, Eric Klein, was hypnotized and inspired by Cunningham before he won the 1977 World Championship in archery.

Late in the 1979 Australian soccer season, Marco Jancovics, Australian striker and leading goal scorer in the national competition, suffered a dramatic loss of form. For weeks on end he did not add to his tally of goals. However, after a number of sessions with Cunningham, Jancovics scored three brilliant goals in the following game.

More recently Cunningham worked with the cyclist Gary Sutton, one of Australia's hopefuls for a gold medal at the Moscow Olympics. Sutton claimed to suffer from nervousness and a general lack of confidence as well as feeling jaded from his 60-kilometres-a-day training routine. However, after some personal sessions with Cunningham and the practice of self-hypnosis to some tapes prepared by Cunningham, Sutton rode one of his most forceful and intelligent races in winning the Sydney Thousand.

This handicap race mixed Australia's leading professional and amateur cyclists over 2000 metres. Sutton, after a pre-race session with Cunningham, had to start off scratch and give a handy lead to most of his competitors. Yet, in a perfectly timed race which combined intelligent riding and a blistering finish, he not only gave the others a start he also gave them a good beating. After the race Sutton commented that 'What Les did for me tonight certainly worked. Usually I'm very nervous before a race but tonight I was able to stay calm, gather my wits and put together one of the best races of my career.'

In March 1980 Les Cunningham worked, with great success, with Australian swimmers and cyclists. Of the 20 swimmers named in the Olympic team, 12 had been using Cunningham's tapes for at least two months and Ron McKeon,

Grahame Brewer and Trevor Cracknell all swam season-best times in their events at the Olympic trials. At the Australian Cycling Championships a week later, only three weeks after South Australia broke the Australian record for pursuit teams, Cunningham worked with the New South Wales team and saw them beat South Australia by six seconds.

We could provide a long long list of such successes but space dictates that we must now return to some case studies which show precisely how Cunningham dealt with certain problems and the lessons to be learnt from his experiences. We shall look at two cases in detail: the first concerns Cunningham's involvement with a rowing squad, and the second his intervention to help a basketball team.

Cunningham's involvement with the rowing squad began back in 1974 when John Welch, recently retired from rowing, went to Lucerne, Switzerland, to observe the 1974 World Rowing Championships. Welch intended taking up coaching upon his return to Australia and was very interested in seeing the world's top crews in action. What he saw caused him to think anew about pre-race preparation. He particularly noted the efforts of the East Germans who won five gold medals in the men's events and dominated the women's competition and whose rowers adopted a mask of intense concentration immediately before the start of each event. As he commented in a letter to Cunningham: 'Off-the-water pre-race physical and mental preparation was evident. The capacity of crews, particularly from the East European countries, to concentrate on technique throughout the strain of a race lasting from six to eight minutes without faltering and maintaining even split times for each of the four 500-metre sections requires more than mere physical preparation.'

To the casual observer, rowing appears to be just another power sport: muscles are the key and any rower can excel simply by training hard, rowing further and building bigger and better muscles. As with most casual observations, there is only a grain of truth in that first opinion. Certainly, muscles are important — as they are in any sport — but in top-level rowing competitions the efficient distribution and co-ordination of muscle power, both within the individual and the crew, is essential to keep the boat moving smoothly and quickly. Maintaining the correct style and co-ordination through a long and muscle-jangling race requires intense concentration from each competitor.

Returning to Australia, Welch was appointed Lightweight Coach of the Drummoyne Rowing Club and he was particularly concerned about the performance of the Lightweight IV, who were unable to beat a combination from the Sydney Rowing Club. Welch considered his crew to be both physically and technically superior to the Sydney crew but they seemed to be lacking in self-confidence and the basic will to win. And so began a two-year association between Cunningham, Welch and his rowing crews.

In the first instance the Drummoyne Lightweight IV embarked upon a programme of hypnosis combined with positive thinking and suggestions presented by Cunningham either in person or via a tape recording. Starting this programme three weeks before the State championships, the crew responded well and improved to the point where they beat their Sydney counterparts and won the Resident State Championship.

We now progress to 1976 and Welch is coaching at the Sydney University Boat Club. He has under his charge a group of young oarsmen who are competing in the Second Grade or Junior ranks. Again the most difficult problem, as Welch saw it, was building confidence and negating their own doubts about their abilities. To overcome this problem, Cunningham began working with the crew some six weeks before their first major test.

Early sessions were devoted to mapping out a course for the season's activities — emphasizing hard training and the correct style — culminating in competition victories on the way to the Australian championships. Throughout these early sessions the constantly recurring theme was that the team, and the individuals had the power plus the ability to develop that power even further when it was combined with the knowledge and experience of one of the best coaches in Australia. In this way they would eventually be transformed into the best team in Australia. This two-pronged attack which was aimed at developing the individual's faith in himself as well as the coach, paid early dividends.

According to Welch, improvements in all team members

were obvious after only two or three sessions. The whole crew took to training with renewed gusto and listened more carefully and faithfully to his instructions. However, the most notable improvements were seen in the individual's work output as measured on a rowing ergometer. With a fresh concept of their own ability, several members of the squad were able to break that magic barrier of 1000 ergs for the first time and three members in particular lifted their work output by over 70 ergs to achieve the once impossible 1000 ergs of manpower.

In their preparation for the New South Wales championships, Cunningham again conducted sessions with the crew and helped prepare them for some important races in Victoria. Unfortunately the team took along their reserve boat and it was just not up to the strength of the team. In the first race, the Founder's Challenge Cup, the crew was well away and in the lead when a seat broke. In the second race, the Grand Challenge Cup, the Sydney University crew was leading by two lengths with only 400 metres to go, when a seat slide broke away. The rower who suffered the broken slide jumped overboard and even though the crew was down one oar, the race was lost only in the last twenty strokes. As could be imagined, such misfortune and displays of persistence under adversity gave Cunningham a fertile psychological field to play with: 'If you can nearly win with seven, imagine what you can do with a full eight. . . You guys are out on your own.'

Further sessions during the following week, combined with an early morning confidence booster and a pre-start pep-talk, saw the University crew, in the words of a newspaper report, 'outclass' all their opposition and become the top Second (or Junior) Grade eight-oar crew in New South Wales. The following week the same crew stunned officials when they stroked their way to a win over the hot favourites, Mosman (whose crew contained six Australian representatives), to win the prestigious Riverview Gold Cup—a race, incidentally, which was open to both senior and junior crews. The win was not without drama, however, since the Sydney University side lost to Mosman in a semi-final and looked as if they could easily falter in the final. Cunningham intervened in the meantime to bolster their determination and will to win: 'Reputations mean nothing in any sport. Those bastards are only flesh and blood, just like you, but you. . .' And in the final, the University crew was a one-and-a-half lengths better team, winning the race by a record margin and in a record time.

The same squad of rowers then progressed, with intermittent, and sometimes crucial assistance from Cunningham, to win at the 1976 Australian Championships, the second-grade eights, the second-grade fours and the second-grade pairs. As John Welch later commented: 'Never before had one junior squad from the same club been able to achieve victories at the national level, in the eights, fours and pairs in the one year'.

Welch continued his association with Cunningham when he was appointed coach of the New South Wales Colt's Team due to tour New Zealand and perform in two Test races against the top New Zealand Colts Team. As part of the preparation for this tour, the team made an attempt on the world endurance rowing record, and, after several months of physical preparation combined with several sessions of mental preparation, Welch was adamant that the combination of the two was directly responsible for the team being able to endure the pain of rowing 113 miles (182 kilometres) in just under twelve hours and establish the new world record. Cunningham accompanied the New South Wales Colts to New Zealand but a combination of illness and equipment failure saw the New Zealanders beat the New South Welshmen by one second in the first race and by a more substantial margin in the final race, when a seat in the Colts' boat broke under the pressure.

The successes of the rowing teams owe much to good coaching, intelligent tactics, hard work and sound mental preparation, and we are mainly interested in Cunningham's contribution to that mental preparation. Again, the format followed the general lines of Cunningham's involvement with football teams and was a condensed version of the scenario we outline in our chapter on suggestion and mental progress through a sporting season.

In the case of the rowers, at the start of the season the emphasis was on goals and the possibility, ability and then *certainty* of the team members achieving those goals. Here the task was to instil self-confidence into the individual and mould a competitive self-image which said 'I will do it'.

In the more immediate period before the race Cunningham

would conduct individual sessions in the week before and then group sessions either the day before or early on the actual day of the race.

With the individual sessions Cunningham would attempt to orient and motivate the rower towards the upcoming race: 'You've come so far, worked so hard and now the big race is coming up. It's your golden opportunity to grasp it and become a champion. . .' He would also run through general images of rowing and the correct style for that particular individual — emphasizing certain points that Welch felt needed either concentration on or correcting. The following examples are points that Cunningham introduced into the psyche of a second grade IV through hypnotic suggestion, and these suggestions relate mainly to the development of the correct style of rowing:

Dave   smooth finish and wind; no pausing at front chocks; clean catch, in time; controlled steady rowing.

Chris   sit back, finish the stroke smoothly and cleanly; open up from catch.

Steve   hold finish in squarely; smooth finish and wind; sit up, chest out, at finish of stroke.

Tim   sit up tall at finish; draw finishes up and wind.

With the team assembled, Cunningham would conduct a group induction, often using a tape recording. Cutting in at an appropriate time, he would run through a range of confidence-boosting suggestions and then get on to the specifics of the race plan. Encouraging the crew to mentally rehearse the race, Cunningham would describe the race that Welch had planned: 'OK you boys, we come to the start together, blasting out hard and clean, concentrating, applying yourself to your strokes. . . thinking only about how far you can move the boat with each stroke. . . and you wind up perfectly until you have reached your optimum rate by the tenth stroke. . . and you're away. . . stroking powerfully and purposely, feeling like you're part of the boat — like a well-oiled, finely tuned powerful motor, running perfectly and making your boat glide along fast and smoothly. . .

'And through the body of the race you settle down to the powerful, relaxed long rhythm of a beautiful motor, concentrating all the time on your catch timing and your lively

legs. . . Through this period you will respond to any efforts
called by Brian (the cox) by an increase in the power of your
stroke rather than by increasing the stroke rate . . . at the 1600
metre mark Brian will call "wind-up" and on this signal you will
increase the pressure and let the stroke rate climb, still
powerful, relaxed and purposeful, stroking powerfully right
through to the finish and victory.'

Immediately before the race Cunningham would hypnotize
the crew and, with all the rowers strewn around him, begin a
final pepping-up: 'You fellows are big race rowers and all the
training and racing you have done this season has been part of
a schedule to bring you up to that big race form. And today's
the day that the wraps come off. This is the day that you have
been working for and you're going to grab that championship
because it belongs to you.

'You boys have got tons going for you. You have more big
race experience in your team than in the rest of the finalists put
together.

'You have got more ability than the rest of the finalists put
together.

'You have got the best coach in the business.

'You have got the best cox in the business.

'And you will row today as though you were rowing for
Australia—your co-ordination with your team-mates will be
the best it's ever been, your strokes will be. . .'

And so into the water.

The success of the rowing teams coached by John Welch is
attributable to the professional approach of the coach himself
and his careful co-ordination of physical and mental
preparation throughout the season. This success emphasizes
once again the point that the physical, mental and tactical
inputs into any sport cannot be separated. It is essential that
they all mesh and, provided the fit is good, success is a very
reasonable proposition. The role of hypnosis in this process is
not that of a magic wand. Hypnosis will never transform a
motley bunch of ignorant, unfit and ill-guided individuals into
a successful performance unit. But hypnosis *can* fix goals and
the determination to reach those goals; hypnosis *can* be used to
mentally rehearse the individual and team in the style and
tactics necessary to achieve those goals; and, finally, hypnosis
can be used to develop the correct arousal level so essential for

that final success. It is no magic wand, rather it is a very thoughtful approach to success in a very competitive arena. Professionalism is the key and the story below provides a further example of the importance of a professional approach to competitive sport.

Basketball in Australia has really blossomed only since the formation, in 1979, of the National Invitation Basketball League when clubs from all over Australia were organized into a competition. The club which is our main concern in this section, the Canberra Cannons, applied to join this competition but their application met strong opposition from senior officials and other clubs in the league. Their main concern was that Canberra basktball was not up to the national standard and that too few people would pay to see the Cannons in action. However, through compromise and practicability — Canberra's entry made up an even ten teams while its geographic position placed it in a convenient central location for 'away' games — the entry of the Canberra Cannons was accepted.

Hardly an auspicious entry — there to make up the numbers and expected to bottom-out and win the first wooden spoon of the competition. Yet this same team went on to earn the title of 'Cinderella' of the competition. And a large part of this transformation was due to the influence of captain-coach, Cal Stamp.

Stamp was recruited by the Canberra administration soon after the acceptance of the Cannon's entry to the National League. He flew in from the United States to become the local Director of Coaching and captain-coach of the Cannons. Stamp's first and primary concern was to build up and weld together a competitive unit and, as one means to this end, he consulted Cunningham on the psychological approach he should adopt.

Stamp, with a 6 foot 9 inch (202.5 centimetre), 215 pound (97 kilogram) physique, would appear to have the ideal body for basketball, but he attributes a large part of his success to the mental rehearsal that he engages in before each game: 'I don't think I was born gifted with an athletic ability but because I was able to use my basic physical talents and combine them with a good mental approach, I was able to succeed'.

The mental rehearsal practised by Stamp simply involved shutting himself away in a quiet room for 30 minutes, any time up to four hours before a game. Relaxed and as comfortable as possible, Stamp would play the whole game through, imagining himself in the positions he had been instructed to adopt. According to Stamp there is no way that a player can simply arrive at a venue and then say to himself: 'I'll now concentrate on this game and psyche myself up for it'. This will never work because the mental priming has to occur long before the event.

The result of such mental practice saw Stamp become the most 'in-demand' player in the Atlantic Coast Conference in America — averaging only 1.5 minutes per game on the reserve's bench. In addition his mistake rate dropped dramatically, to only one or two per game. When he arrived in Australia to take up his first serious coaching position, he was determined to adopt a similar approach.

Using one of Cunningham's tapes (script 2 in Chapter 11), Stamp assembled his team and explained to them why he was using the tape and then related his own successes through using mental rehearsal. He then played the tape through and when the players were totally relaxed he encouraged them to imagine the course of the coming game and their role in that play. With an emphasis around the development of a team spirit and the role of the individual within the team, the players went through the game from warm-up to victory, seeing themselves playing correctly and in accord with all the moves they had practised in training.

Stamp used this tape and approach during the first four games, which were all 'away' games. Isolated from local support and with players who had little experience of playing together as a team, these games, according to Stamp, were the most crucial of the competition: 'The result could make or break the team'.

The results in these crucial games were four straight wins, with the Cannons maintaining their initial momentum to win their next three games and lead the competition, as well as astound the critics. After a number of mid-season losses the Cannons finish the season with thirteen wins from their eighteen games and, with their second placing in the competition, were due to meet the 'glamour' side, St. Kilda Pumas, to decide the top team in Australia.

The St. Kilda team were deservedly regarded as the top team in the competition — after a slow start, when they lost three of their first five games, they 'put it all together' to win all of their thirteen remaining games; beating the Cannons twice in the process, by margins of eighteen and five points. And, after their recovery from the early season losses, the Pumas in both State and National competition won over thirty games — and here is an illustration of how complacency can beset any team — losing only one game, and that to the lowest placed team in the Victorian State competition.

The St. Kilda team was basically the Australian team, with four of their five 'first-up' players national representatives. Coached by former Australian Olympian, Brian Kerle, the St Kilda side was as formidable an opponent as anyone could wish for in a grand final.

As part of the Cannons' preparation for the final, Stamp enlisted Cunningham's assistance. The format of Cunningham's involvement followed earlier examples; individual sessions combined with a group session immediately before the game and again at half-time. Because of the twin factors of time and distance, both individual and group sessions had to be compressed into the morning of the grand final day.

Stamp outlined a list of general points he wanted emphasized to the whole team plus some specific instructions for each player. The theme which permeated Stamp's thoughts on the game was the need to be tight and rugged in defence. St. Kilda was renowned as the fastest breaking team in Australia; whenever they had the chance, a fast passing, rushing wall of players would suddenly be down at the other end and shooting, usually successfully, into their opponent's goal. It was essential that this pattern of play be broken up. And because of this, images of a cat — prowling, stalking, harassing, always crouched low (an essential feature of a defensive style in basketball) intruded into much of the suggestion used by Cunningham.

We will deal with only two of the individual sessions because these two examples effectively illustrate the points we have made about the crucial role of suggestion and its relevance to each subject. The first example concerns Jim Cotta, an Australian who had honed his basketball skills in a four-year stint in Canada. Cotta was an important cog in the Cannon's point-scoring machinery and it was essential that he have a big game. Since he was also in line for selection in the Australian Olympic side, he had a strong personal interest in performing well. Such a suggestion began the list Cunningham used:

'Jim. . . Today you will have a big game, a game that will enhance your chances of selection in the Olympic squad—and today you are going to play your way into that squad.

'To achieve this end you are going to get right out in the open, thrusting forward, going straight up and shooting for goal. Your timing, judgement and accuracy will be at a peak.

'Don't worry about dribbling, just thrust up the middle, because your job is to shoot goals—especially when you are wide open because you are especially good when you are wide open.

'And if you happen to miss a shot the only effect it will have is to make your concentration sharper on following shots'.

This last suggestion was included since Stamp considered that Cotta became very unsettled by mistakes.

The second example involved Jerry Lee, an American whose aggressive defence was essential to the Cannons. Stamp was particularly worried that, in the big-game atmosphere, Lee could continually overstep the mark and foul himself out of the game—a loss which the Cannons could ill-afford. Accordingly, Cunningham emphasized the need for Lee to be a 'smart' cat in his play.

'Jerry, your defence is excellent but you are worth more on the court than off it. You can afford to sacrifice the occasional two points because your defence and general play is worth at least three times this. This is called playing smart and being a smart cat.

'And remember that you can always recover any conceded points by quick, fast play off any rebounds and getting that ball moving straight up the middle again. And in this case you can be as aggressive as you want to be and there is no need to foul-out. Be smart.'

After all ten players in the team had undergone their individual sessions (and received individual suggestions) the whole team assembled and Cunningham conducted a group session—again using the tape as an induction medium. He ran through the general instructions prepared by Stamp. We quote directly from a tape recording of this session, beginning when the players were in a totally relaxed and susceptible state of mind:

'You guys started this season really well and you confounded all of your critics and now we're into the grand final — and this is what we're talking about — a grand final. There are people who have played basketball all their lives and never get to play in a grand final — and you're going to confound them some more today because when you first started the season you had the tape to listen to a couple of times and I reckon that must have helped you a little bit but today, boys, you've got the master himself here and I'll tell you what, that's good for at least fifteen points.

'Last time you played this mob, St. Kilda, you played one of the best games you ever played but you lost by five points, well you learned all about those bastards in that game. You picked out what they can do, what they can't do and how they do it. You're going to remember that before you go on that court today and, automatically, you will know exactly what you've got to do, who you've got to watch and what sort of play they do. But you'll know what their measure is and you'll know just what you've got to produce.

'And you're going to gain those extra points by grabbing that ball and treating it like a $10 000 bundle of notes. Because that's what it's worth to you today, not to mention the prestige of being Australian champions — it's all in your hands today. And you're going to do it today. Just think of that. By tonight you fellows are going to be Australian champions.

'Once you have that ball you'll be totally in control, loose and sharp, swinging the ball from end to end. Waiting for an open basket which will give you a good shot — then whip that ball into the basket.

'Most of the time work the ball inside to Cal but go for your shots when you see the opportunity and bang!. . . Fellows, you're not going to lose any opportunities out there today.

'On defence — if you miss a shot get back in defence quickly. Sprint as hard as you can and keep your eye on your man. Now he's your responsibility. No rests. No slack time today. You've had all season to get fit and now today all that training, all that hard work will come out today. It's all been worthwhile because you'll really produce the effort today. You're going to find that extra bit of energy from under your toenails — you're going to find sheer guts and stamina you never thought you had before — and it's all going to come out today boys.

'Be tight in defence and always watch where you are, where

the ball is and where the man you're guarding is. He's your responsibility.

'Remember that old saying: think with your mind, move with your feet. Those feet are built for moving and today you're going to move those bastards.

'And as the ball gets further away from your basket, draw off from your man in case he cuts. Then you'll be in position to cut him off and hold him out.

'Keep talking all the time. If you lose your man and want someone to help you recover — yell it out — "screen right, screen left" — and one of your mates will help.

'You are going to be like a cat in defence. A very smart cat, always crouching low and always ready to spring. Always thinking, harassing your man, prowling all around him but never fouling him — because we don't want to give away any silly points.

'You will spring for the ball off the rebound like a cat going for a bird. And like a cat, all you need to do is get a hand to the ball and you've got it.

'And once you have that ball you are in control. Loose and sharp. Getting those baskets whenever you can.

(And as a late addition by Stamp:) 'On the rebound you'll block the guy out, step right into the man on the rebound. If you can't feel him you're not doing it right.

'All the things you know how to do well you're going to do just that little bit better today. You're going to put it all together today.

'I've heard losers say that winning isn't everything in a whinging type of voice. You can tell the bastards have never won anything in their lives — and I'll agree with them — winning isn't everything. It's the only thing. And that's what you've come down here for today: to win!

'And you're not going to be sold short. . .'

Finishing off with general appeals to perform for the sake of mothers, fathers, supporters and coach, Cunningham wound up the session with a final suggestion to enter an even more deeply relaxed state when he hypnotized them next. The team was brought out of the trance, jumped into a series of cars, and headed off to the stadium.

Immediately before the Cannons were due on court, the team was put under hypnosis again to give them a final two-

Australian soccer striker Marco Jancovics. After a loss of form in 1979 he was helped by hypnotherapy and scored three goals in his next match.

Leading cyclist Gary Sutton complained of nervousness, lack of confidence and being jaded. Self-hypnosis and Les Cunningham helped him overcome these problems and produce his most dazzling performances.

minute rousting. At half-time, Cunningham again hypnotized the team, who then listened to summaries of what they had done right, where they had gone wrong and what they should do to correct these faults, from their bench-coach, Terry Ryan and from Stamp himself. Cunningham finished off this session with another basic energy boost along the lines of 'You'll find energy in places where you never knew it existed'. And, as final input, he quickly hypnotized and spurred on individual players when they were resting on the reserve's bench during the second half.

The result of the game? After an even first half during which the Cannons' cat-like defence looked particularly effective, the St. Kilda team jumped to the lead with a scoring rush during the last two minutes, to leave the Cannons in their usual position at half-time when they were down 47-53.

Early in the second-half, the St. Kilda team scored repeatedly to stretch their lead to twelve points but the Cannons stormed home to level the scores with six minutes to go. And from this point the lead changed repeatedly until, with 25 seconds to go, Ian Ellis shot what everyone expected to be the winning goal. The response of the St. Kilda team was to storm down the court. But all their star players were effectively blocked out and could not get into a scoring position. Finally, the ball was passed to St. Kilda's Peter Vitols, who had spent most of the game on the reserves bench. With three seconds to go he knew he had to go for a shot, and did. Driving along the baseline he jumped, stretched and hooked a shot back over his head and into the basket to produce the final score, in St. Kilda's favour, of 94-93.

A win is a win whether its by one point and three seconds or a more substantial margin. However, the Cannons, · their supporters and Cunningham didn't know how to accept the result of the game. They certainly hadn't won, so the champagne didn't deserve to flow. But, in the same breath, they felt as though they hadn't really lost. They had played their best game ever and had come within seconds of beating what was considered to be an unbeatable combination. And such a loss did not warrant a drowning of sorrows in beer. There was a fine tension in the air after that game. How did Vitols get through? He had only scored a few points against the Cannons in their previous encounters. Why did he have to get those vital two points? It is worth asking whether this fact, conceived in a split-second flash, during those final tense seconds, led the Cannons' defenders into the complacent idea that Vitols would pass to one of the star-shooters? But this is unanswerable. Perhaps they should have been prepared for a harder line against the lesser stars in the St Kilda line-up?

There are some other lessons to be learnt from this game and here we refer to the individual sessions with Cotta and Lee, mentioned above. First Cotta, by his own admission, felt really terrible about his own play. Although feeling good and really 'spiked-up' to play well and jump high, he played his lowest scoring game of the season — getting only seven points when he usually scored around twenty. In addition he was relatively sluggish in defence and Vitols was the man he was supposed to be blocking out. A very unhappy game for Cotta and we must ask whether the hypnotic suggestion he experienced was responsible for this.

Amidst a whole host of imponderables which surface whenever a champion performs below his best, it is worth considering whether Cotta could really identify with the cat-like images he experienced, or whether 'thrusting' was an appropriate term to describe what was expected of him or, finally, whether Cotta, after a four year absence from Australia, subconsciously did not really wish to make it into the Olympic team and go off on another overseas trek? One other point which helped shade-out Cotta's performance in the second-half was that the players slavishly obeyed the instruction to work the ball inside to Cal' which, when the chips were down in the second-half left Cotta few opportunities to score: he only touched the ball a few times. Lack of ball, lack of scoring opportunities and the resultant frustration don't make for a happy player.

Such things do occur and these questions and problems surrounding the use of suggestions are worth considering. The maturity and personality of the athlete and their interaction with any suggestion is worthy of deep consideration. We make this point specifically for zealous or achieving school teachers and dads.

In contrast, many athletes obviously identify with the hypnotic suggestions presented to them. As an example consider the case of the weightlifter in Chapter 8 who took his 'life and death' suggestions quite literally. Jerry Lee appeared to be another athlete who struck a suggestion pattern compatible with his good performance. First, his defence was as rugged and as effective as usual. He broke up the St Kilda attack single-handedly several times. Second, despite being the subject of some questionable calls, he played within his limits and fouled out only in the last minute of the game. Third, he made up for 'pulling his punches', as suggested by Cunningham, by scoring seventeen points, his best score for the season and well above his usual tally of six to seven points a game.

Overall, Cunningham's involvement did not provide the fifteen points he promised, but it did make up the major part of the five point deficit suffered in the previous St Kilda-Cannons clashes. Whether careful analysis of each player's requirements, as detailed in the case below, would have helped; whether a week of psychological preparation involving less haste and more careful formulation of suggestions, would be worth a final-clinching six points, are just more imponderables.

We shall now detail a case taken from the pages of *Research Quarterly*, published in the United States by the American Association for Health, Physical Education and Recreation. We can do no better than quote it directly and feel that you will be able to cope with the few instances of jargon. It is by Warren R. Johnson, of the University of Maryland, titled: 'Body Movement Awareness in the Nonhypnotic and Hypnotic States'

This case is reported because it is suggestive of an extensive body movement awareness which is apparently not ordinarily accessible to conscious verbal representation. Moreover, this case would seem to have some interesting implications for Henry's nonconscious memory drum theory of neuromotor control of movements.

A baseball player who had volunteered to serve in an exercise physiology visual hallucinations, etc.)

While in the nonhypnotic state, the subject tried unsuccessfully to describe just what had gone wrong with his batting. He was then asked to enter a deep hypnotic trance and in this state was instructed to analyse his batting problem. Again he tried but was puzzled and frustrated by the effort.

He was then told that the investigator would present a signal which would elicit spontaneous verbalization. The signal was that the investigator would count to ten slowly and then rap on his desk. The subject was instructed to make no effort to analyse his batting problems but merely to sit and think of nothing. (It is emphasized that the investigator made no suggestions or comments to the subject which might have guided the analysis described here. It is also pointed out that the investigator at no time watched the subject play baseball.)

The signal was given. A few moments later the subject began to analyse his stance and batting movements. (The look of incredulity on the subject's face, as he talked, suggested that he was as surprised by what he had to say as the investigator was.) Starting with feet and legs, he took into account his pelvis, his arms, his grip on the bat, his swing, and his eyes. In each instance he named specific errors of timing, co-ordination, or position as the case might be. When asked if he would now be able to correct the mistakes which had given rise to the deterioration of his batting, he seemed confident that he would be able to do so.

He was then asked which would be better, to experience full conscious recall of his analysis posthypnotically or to have this knowledge just come to him as he practised and played. Presently he stated that it would be better for it to come to him in time rather than to recall it posthypnotically.

The subject's batting performance improved immediately. And, indeed, he finished the season with a 0.400 average. He had by then acquired the reputation of being one of the best players in the region.

At the close of the season he returned to the investigator, giving him full credit for his comeback and success. He was asked whether he remembered what took place during the hypnotic session. He had not remembered it immediately afterwards, he said, but subsequently, it had come back to him. When asked just what had come to him, he stated that he remembered the investigator's analysis of what he was doing wrong in each specific movement and how he was using his eyes incorrectly; he said he remembered receiving hypnotic suggestions as to just how to correct his various mistakes. The subject found the explanation of what had actually happened difficult to believe until he was reminded that the investigator had never seen him play and could not possibly have been able to diagnose the problem or prescribe its solution.

Three points seem especially interesting in this case. 1. The subject's awareness of his movements and just what was wrong with them was detailed and readily verbalized under the special conditions established in the hypnotic state. Furthermore, if one may judge by the sudden improvement and persisting excellence of performance and by the coach's report to the investigator, the analysis was correct. 2. It would seem that the subject showed insight when he elected not to remember consciously the analysis of his motor skill, in that over-consciousness of complex movements seems to affect performance adversely. 3. Although posthypnotic amnesia obliterated out-of-trance awareness of what took place in the trance, in due course the subject "filled in" his memory in terms of his expectations regarding the session.

10
SUGGESTION AND IMAGINATION

This chapter on self or auto-suggestion is designed to be used in conjunction with the following chapter on self-hypnosis and the scripts provided in that chapter. In previous chapters we have elaborated on the meaning of that old adage which says that 'You become what you think you are' and its crucial role in the manipulation of thoughts and functions by hypnosis. And by now you should be aware of the importance of relaxation, imagery and imagination in the development of the self-image. This chapter is basically a guide to the use of hypnotic suggestion to manipulate self-image in the psychological preparation and priming of an athlete for competition.

In the same way that we have stated and shown that you 'become what you think you are' so we have also stated in the course of this book that 'The will always breaks before muscle' and the related fact: 'Imagination always dominates the will'. And when you get down to it the crucial input into hypnosis, after relaxation, is the use of imagination. And you manipulate imagination, you manipulate the hypnotic routine, you manipulate your psychological input into sport through the use of suggestion.

The crucial input into hypnosport is suggestion and for a simple demonstration of the power of suggestion, consider the experience of the advertising world which has long recognized this power and takes advantage of a suggestible consumer population every time it tries to sell the latest soap powder, food or car. Indeed, one of the basic creeds of the advertising man is the injunction 'to sell the sizzle not the steak'—the aroma and prospects of a fine steak are much more appealing to the consumer than any of the other drab pieces of information associated with a hunk of muscle. They sell cars and soap powders in much the same way. We intend to guide your imagination and fantasies so that you become your own advertiser — selling yourself and your form and prospects to yourself. Until you salivate automatically at the prospect of each new competition encounter.

As the last sentence suggests, we are strongly influenced by Pavlov's conditioning theories and the picture we are about to paint is built around the need for continual practice and reinforcement. This picture is composed of three parts. The first part describes our *ideal* plan for the psychological preparation, development and progress of a potential champion through a competition season. The second section covers the general aspects of sport and provides suggestions relating to various competition situations. The third part relies on you. We have already given you various suggestions and ideas relating to the psychological inputs of sport and it is now up to you to apply these ideas. We hope you will have seen routines and ideas applicable to you and will now use these routines to improve your sporting excellence.

Our first section concerns a plan for a potential champion and we labour under the handicap of knowing that not every reader wants, or expects, to be a champion. Most people know their limitations or have more dominant interests than sport, whether it be families, studies or work. However, these readers can still expect to benefit from the descriptions of long and short-term preparation and the recommendations associated with these aspects of competition. In addition, many readers will recognize flaws in their own game which are amenable to the psychological conditioning described in the preparation of our ideal champion. Finally, the development of that most important attribute, the competition mentality with its nebulous qualities of goal orientation, grim determination and the will to win, can be translated from sports into everyday life. It is our hope that in this plotting of our imaginary champion's progress we will show how the development and practice of certain patterns of thought can be applied both in the sporting arena and in the more general tournament of life.

So you want to be a Champion
The starting point for any championship endeavour comes with the realization that sporting success is a pyramid built on the

triangular base of physical conditioning, psychological conditioning and intelligence. All three corners of the triangle impinge on and influence one another in the construction of the pyramid and it is only when the three corners are in fine harmony that they mesh to form the peak. Upon that peak the word 'champion' blazes as a measure of that successful harmony.

The logical place to start in the construction of that pyramid is at the triangle point labelled 'intelligence'. First-off, get yourself a good coach. He will provide you with some of the most important intelligence you will need in your quest. Ideally this coach should have a good track record of producing top-class competitors and should be some one you trust and respect for their knowledge. Sit down and discuss with him your ideas and prospects for the season and, together, plot out the training and competition schedules necessary for you to· realize your ambitions. Once these schedules are set, stick to them. This is your first and most crucial exercise in self-discipline; a discipline which you must maintain right throughout the competition season. Fail at first base and your ability to realize your ambitions will be warped. This should be obvious to you.

Right. You have set yourself a goal and have mapped out a path towards that goal. At all times maintain your orientation towards this goal and let nothing divert you, because as far as you are concerned nothing else is important. Now comes the hard work.

The importance of the second leg of the triangle, physical conditioning, is so obvious that it hardly needs stating. But in the pre-season build-up to a competition the obvious is often forgotten. Let us restate the obvious: a good strong man will always beat an equally good but slightly weaker opponent. In the final crunch of any competition, other things being equal, the individual or team with the greatest endurance will finally dominate. The attitude of the would-be champion has to be radically different from that of the occasional or weekend competitor who plays sport to get fit. The champion's credo is 'Get fit to play sport'.

There are also some less obvious but equally important advantages to getting fit in pursuit of that ultimate goal. Being fit makes actual game practice easier and the athlete is able to practise harder and longer; a second advantage is that the progression of increasing muscular strength, power and endurance provides an obvious demonstration that the champion is making progress along the path that has been mapped out. Such demonstrations can have positive reinforcing effects on the athlete's progress and can be manipulated, as we outlined below, to encourage the athlete to harder and greater endeavours.

Programming the mind

As with any computer,the quality of the programme and the eventual working out of that programme, are only as good as the inputs. The brain is no different.

Not only do the inputs need to be of high quality, they also need to follow a regular order. They have to be logical as well as to the point. Once such a programme is fed to the human bio-computer and accepted, it remains on permanent stand-by and can be activated whenever it is desired. This is the ultimate development of that competition mentality.

The quality of the inputs is dependent on the specific suggestions and the clarity of the images associated with them. The order of the inputs can be categorized as long-term, medium and short-term, competition activation and the post-competition let-down. These stages all merge and intrude into each other. A description of each stage and the inputs relevant to each stage, follows. These descriptions are directed to you and your ambitions.

Long-term Preparations

The simplest description of this stage is that it is a stage concerned with your goal orientation.

Well before the season starts—weeks before—you should start using the self-hypnosis routines we described in Chapter 11 and use these techniques to concentrate on your ultimate goal—the championship—and imagine with crystal clarity, the points on the pathway you have mapped out.

Several points deserve emphasis:

At no time should any negative thoughts or doubts be allowed to intrude into your imaginings. The only things that should be thought of are the positive steps towards the championship. Visions of the crowd, the arena, the sights, sounds and smells, your role in the winning play, the championship-winning performance, the applause and euphoria associated with victory. . . should be all that concerns you at this stage in your preparation.

This goal orientation stage should be developed during the pre-season, before any contests or tests of your ability have been made. And during this period when you are training hard, getting fit to play your sport, you should tune in on your body. Even when you are in the totally relaxed state of self-hypnosis you can imagine the arching, tensing and flexing of limbs and muscles. You can actually feel and see the strength, power and endurance attainable through hard training. You can see progress all the time—in the number of push-ups you can perform, the distance you can run—and the continuing progress of your physical conditioning confirms your belief in your championship-winning abilities. See yourself getting tauter, tighter, fitter all the time, until you are bubbling over with energy at that final championship contest.

Such thoughts and imaginings should be practised at least three times a week during pre-season training but, as we mentioned above, the various stages in psychological preparation merge and intrude into one another and the attitudes associated with long-term preparation should be the greatest mergers and intruders. It is always wise to keep your goal in mind and use the images of that goal to refresh your memory when, for example, you are feeling jaded from heavy training. Renew your enth siasm, convince yourself that it is all worthwhile by getting a fresh focus on your long-term goals. At other times, after an important victory, for example, it pays to enliven your psyche with images of what you plan to achieve. Goal orientation, goal reinforcement and goal seeking are the basis of the long-term strategy.

Medium and Short-term Strategy

The medium term in competition preparation takes in the training period before a contest; it is of variable length.

The short term covers the immediate period one to seven days before the contest. It is difficult to define and separate these pre-competition periods where practice, training and learning all merge.

Medium-term preparation involves the practice and perfection of the correct style—whether it be running, catching, batting, flexing or stroking. It is a period of generalities when the basics of the sport are practised over and over again. It is also a period when the physical training is stepped-up in anticipation of reaching a peak just before the contest.

The short-term period is the time when the coach and athlete get down to specifics — critically examining and analysing the opposition and formulating game-plans. If the athlete's style is deficient in one aspect of the game-plan, it is also a period when practice and perfection, often only of one aspect of play, is emphasized again. In the same vein, the game-plan has to be practised, so learning intrudes for the first time. It is also the time when the athlete should have come close to physical perfection or is maintaining that condition.

A final and very important psychological intrusion into the short-term preparation is the appearance of stage fright. This may appear days or even hours before the start of the contest and the symptoms — tension, restlessness, insomnia and the loss of memory — can undo all the good lead-up work. These symptoms, being of psychosomatic origin, are amenable to treatment.

The integration of self-suggestion into the medium and short-term preparation can be categorized into the three components mentioned above: practice, learning and stage fright. Your imaginings should run as follows.

Practice

During this period when you are trying to perfect your style, your self-suggestions should reflect the style you are aiming for. You should listen to your coach's advice on this matter. If you have access to a videotape recorder, it is even better to have your coach show you recordings of where you are playing correctly and where · you are wrong and then focus your imagination on the 'right' style. Imagine video recordings of yourself running, catching, batting, flexing, or stroking, with the perfect co-ordination and style of a true champion.

It doesn't really matter if you don't have access to a video recorder. The important point is that you see yourself playing as you wish to play. And you can be as specific as you like, indeed, this is a time for specifics. For example, the correction of a poor grip on a bat or a tennis racquet is aided immeasurably by focusing your mind on a picture of the bat or racquet sitting correctly in your hand. Feel its texture and weight, feel the power of your grip — it's just right — and then play imaginary strokes. Similarly, you can concentrate on your footwork, hand and eye co-ordination, and breathing. In fact any of the inputs into your sport, no matter how trifling or esoteric they may be, can benefit by feeding the correct detail into your subconscious. And even if your training and practice is progressing perfectly, there is no harm in reinforcing this progression by seeing yourself running harder, hitting the ball harder, retrieving extremely difficult balls, always pushing yourself to the limits of an imagined perfection.

These sessions of self-suggestion should continue regularly, at least twice a week, and more often if it is necessary to correct a range of faults. Only *one* should be tackled at each session. Do not crowd your subconscious with too many images. You know you work best when all your energies are centred on one problem; the same applies to your subconscious. The number of sessions devoted to a problem is quite arbitrary and here feedback from your coach is essential. Look to him for a measure of your improvement and plan from there. One, two, three, six or more sessions may be necessary, depending on the nature of the problem.

We have mentioned the problems of 'over-training'. Whenever you feel tired and you start to wonder whether the effort is worth it, when there are other things which are capturing your attention — let your imagination wander again along the path to the championship and experience the euphoria and trappings of victory. Refresh your memory with your long-term aim. Then all the slog of training will appear worthwhile and you will find you can take to it with renewed zeal.

Learning

We learn best when we are relaxed. And from the carefully paced swim through to the elaborate tactics of gridiron, there is always something to be learnt in sport. The best approach to the problem of learning is to practise relaxation and then focus all your attention on the words of your coach. Then run through the scenes the coach is describing in your imagination. Get the coach's words on tape if possible and listen to them again in the relaxing quiet of your own home. Study any diagrams or films again as if you had only just seen them and then see yourself actually playing in the contest to the plan. Go over it again and again — not in the sense of learning it by rote, but actually playing to the plan.

Stagefright

It is natural for an athlete to feel tense before a big contest and we deal with the problem of pre-contest tension in detail below. Our main concern in this section is the most debilitating aspect of stagefright, the phenomenon of insomnia, a problem which can sap the carefully cultivated energy of any athlete with disastrous results.

Our approach to this problem is along the lines of 'forewarned is forearmed'. A mental rehearsal of all the penultimate day's events helps you to adjust to them; since you have anticipated the days events there is nothing unusual which can possibly unsettle you.

Approximately a week before the contest you should start imagining all the details of the preparation necessary for the contest. See, in vivid detail, the events of the day before the contest. If possible you should plan a routine in advance — work or study, a light meal, a bit of reading or TV and then bed. Even if it involves travel, you can still mentally rehearse the events as you expect them to occur on the day. See yourself going through the routine you have set for yourself. Imagine what you will be eating on that night. Imagine the pleasant feelings of tiredness and the pleasant expectations of the next day. Imagine yourself yawning and experience the need to recharge your batteries — because tomorrow all that energy is going to flood out in an unbeatable surge. See yourself going to bed; feel the texture of the sheets and the warm, enveloping heaviness of the blankets. See yourself having a good night's sleep and literally jumping out of the bed the next morning because you are so full of energy, freshly bottled-up after such a good night's sleep. You can hardly wait for the day's events to start.

On another tack, if sleep evades you, use your capacity for self-hypnosis to relax yourself. The self-suggestion should be confined solely to images of relaxation. Think of descending elevators, warm baths, sunbathing on a pleasantly warm day or any other relaxing image you find appealing. Focus your imagination on these images and don't allow any other thoughts to intrude. If they do, focus your attention on one particular aspect of your relaxing image. For instance, see your toe sticking out of the warm bath water, look at it closely, see the texture of the nails and the colour of your skin and hairs. Concentrate on that toe for a moment and then draw back, very slowly, until you can see the whole of your body immersed in the relaxing warmth of that bath. Then concentrate again on the feelings associated with that bath.

Another approach is a variant on the old counting sheep routine. This technique involves relaxing yourself through self-hypnosis and then concentrating on your breathing. Imagine that every breath puts more soothing relaxation into your body and that after every breath you become more and more relaxed. Silently repeat the word 'one' after every breath, the purpose of the word being to concentrate your attention on your breathing and the relaxation that is coursing through your body. It doesn't matter if another word besides 'one' is used; any simple word will serve to block out distracting thoughts and concentrate your attention on the relaxation of sleep.

Competition Activation

Here we come to the crunch! This is where the tension arises. It is essential that you manipulate that tension to achieve your ends.

Competition activation starts as soon as you even *think* of the contest in the pre-season. For several weeks you will be thinking of that contest, expecting all your bottled-up energy to bubble-up and explode when it reaches the surface of the arena. But there you are, on the day, and what do you do?

Several hours before, or even right up to the immediate contest start, relax yourself through self-hypnosis. Take last-minute instructions from your coach if necessary, and then, in your mind, run through your vision of how the contest will go. See yourself actively applying all your carefully learnt skills. See yourself playing to the game plan. Marvel at the fine tuning of body and mind, the mobilization of energy and the perfect co-ordination which produces the winning play — exactly as it was predicted in the game plan.

These positive suggestions should be combined with any images which are important to you, such as seeing yourself as a rock-hard, determined competitor who will not be unsettled or deterred if the tide of the game seems to be turning against you. All sports have varying playing styles and if you can summarize the way you want to play in a few poignant words, this can be very useful. Examples include 'serve and volley' (tennis) and 'loop and kill' (table tennis). Bird images could be used in preparation for running and fish images for swimming races. The only criteria is that the words and images are relevant to you and your game.

The duration of the self-hypnosis sessions should be long enough to encompass all the necessary suggestions — usually ten to twenty minutes is ideal. But we recognize that there are situations, such as a knockout competition, where it is impossible to plan ahead and when only five minutes warning is given. Use this time. Get your gear together, thinking only of the contest at hand. Don't respond to, or partake in any idle chit-chat. Just think of the game and how you are going to play and win it. Use the remaining time to indulge in self-hypnosis and unless you have specific suggestions designed to cope with a particular opponent, confine yourself to a few suggestions important to you and your game — 'seeing the ball', 'playing each point on its merits' or 'seeing yourself as a big man, competitive to the end and winning in the end'.

It doesn't matter how long a period of preparation you have or how esoteric or general the suggestions you wish to feed your subconscious mind. Your interest, in any time you have, should be focused on images of yourself playing to and acting out these suggestions. Always see yourself as you want to be, this is the only way to prime and prepare your subconscious mind so that it functions automatically once you hit the competition arena.

Reaching the Correct Arousal Level

In Chapter 6 we described the importance of the phenomenon of arousal and described a technique for manipulating arousal levels. At this stage it would pay to re-read the last few pages of that chapter, in which we emphasize the role of ritual in controlling arousal — a crucial aspect of precompetition activation. We are now talking about the period of less than an hour before the start of the contest.

The importance of ritual in the pre-competition preparation is recognized by most top coaches and is seen in the frequent injunctions to perform a 'special set' of exercises in the immediate period before the contest. We have suggested in an earlier chapter that the significance of these often esoteric exercises lies not so much in the programming and preparation of muscle, but rather in their effect on the mind — directing and arousing it through a simple direction to the task at hand. Such task orientation is crucial to the success of any sporting endeavour. Remember that you started out the season with the completion of a certain task — a championship — as the dominant theme of your life for that period. You should now realize that the completion of that task is accomplished through a plethora of other tasks. These other tasks may range from the onerous burden of running twenty laps of the local oval through to the simple necessity of getting to training on time. One often decisive but onerous task which is often overlooked in the rush to victory, is the simple ritual which is so pivotal in your achievement of this victory — and that is arousal. Always allow some time before the start of a contest for the induction of the correct arousal level.

We would suggest that the time you devote to arousing yourself should be in proportion to the arousal levels presented in the Table on page 89. This means that for low-arousal sports like golf or snooker, the arousal ritual could involve only the indulgence of a few deep breaths and the concentration of the mind on the simple realities of a ball and the way it will swing or bounce. In contrast, in high arousal sports such as football or sprinting, a longer period of time should be spent in arousing oneself. This is derived from that positive feed-back-loop, discussed in Chapter 6, between increasing muscular activity and the arousal of various parts of the conscious mind. In this case the more intense the muscular activity the greater the effect on the arousal centres of the brain. Stressed push-ups, vigorous running on the spot, deep twists to the body (provided they are integrated into a plan for the slow and progressive warming-up of the muscles concerned) are integral parts of the phenomenon of competition arousal for the physically demanding, high-arousal sports.

Yet it doesn't matter whether the exercise is as simple as a touching of the toes or a number of simple flicks of the wrist, your arousal level can be controlled by the ritual of exercise combined with the silent mouthing of key words and the imagination of key colours until you are activated to the required arousal level. You should practise until you can achieve a continuing success by drawing on past experiences to achieve the reinforcement and association of those past arousal levels. You should practise — and we mean practise — arousing yourself during your routine training sessions. During these sessions arouse yourself to the level you consider necessary to beat all the opposition. Practise a ritual of exercise and the silent imagining of key words or colours until the arousal ritual is second nature to you. Then play a game, ruthlessly, as though you were playing for the championship. Your aim should be to condition your arousal response until you are no different from any of Pavlov's salivating dogs who appreciate and/or expect a bone. Your goal is a little more elaborate, but the principle remains the same. Remember: optimum arousal levels mean optimum performances. An optimum performance spells success.

During the actual contest there will certainly be incidents which, through design or accident, will distract you from the task at hand. These incidents could involve simple bad luck, poor umpiring, gamesmanship or plain bad sportsmanship — you will have probably noted that there is a fine line between gamesmanship and unsporting behaviour. However, the overall efffect is still the same: you are unsettled and your arousal level either dips below or soars angrily above your optimum. If this happens, take a pause. Take a deep breath and remember your word or colour. Focus your imagination on it. See the colour, see the action in your word. Then start the contest again. Never allow yourself to be diverted from your goal.

Post-Competition Letdown

For an athlete on the competition trail, particularly for the edgy type of personality in a high arousal sport, it is just as important to psyche the athlete down as it is to psyche them up for the contest. Many people would recognize from their own experience that feelings of competitiveness, excitement, anger and aggression can persist for hours, sometimes even weeks after the event. The highly aroused athlete is often still 'fighting' or 'smoking' long after the event.

Of course, the description above emphasizes an extreme

personality type competing in an extremely tense sport. However, persistent degrees of post-competition tension remain unresolved and pose problems in most sports. Such lingering tension can interfere with the preparation for another contest on the same or next day or may disrupt a tight training schedule. Far too often the athlete seeks solace and release from tension through the agency of alcohol. Certainly alcohol can be viewed as a reward for a job well done, but its negative points should always be kept in mind. In any case, save your rewards until you have won the championship. Then you can drink the best.

To resolve the problem of post-competition tension a relaxation phase is again of positive value. Take five minutes away from the trappings of the competition and use your relaxation abilities to dissolve your tension — seeing the tension dissipating with every breath. Use the brief period of rest and relaxation to restore and energize your jaded muscles — especially if you have further contests coming up. One other important use which can be made of the post-competition relaxation phase is that the successful athlete's abilities and progress towards his goal can be reinforced so that all the hard training in the past, and, more significantly, the hard training in the future, will appear worthwhile and valuable in the eyes of that athlete. In the case of the unsuccessful competitor, reassurance of abilities, not reinforcement, is the key. In both cases an intelligent and sympathetic coach can play an important role through his analysis of what went right and what went wrong.

The successful athlete should take the time to look back to where he came from; look back along the hard path he has carved out to reach his present position. Savour the feelings of success. So far you've done everything right and as far as you can see this will continue until you have attained your goal of the championship. Don't merely imagine winning the championship but know and understand that by following the path you mapped out early in the season, you *will* win the championship.

In the case of the unsuccessful athlete the post-competition letdown is even more important because here we have a situation of unresolved tension combined with frustration. The initial goal has not been achieved; what chance the ultimate goal? 'Am I really only that good that I lose to a second-rater? Am I only a third-rater?'

Questions, anger, doubts and frustration — losing provokes a confusing mish-mash of emotions and the only way to clarify them is through relaxation. Relax yourself and reflect, calmly, on the events of the day. Perhaps, at the time, the reasons for your loss are not obvious, but no matter, the reasons will out through the critical analysis and support of your coach. At this stage simple relaxation and calm reflection with its soothing and recuperative effects is far better for you than a random gnashing of teeth and angry recollections or an escape to the bottle. And it is worth remembering that surveys of great athletes have shown that they do not dwell upon their losses. Instead, they concentrate upon that part of their performance which limited the achievement of their normal excellence. If it is possible to single out one aspect of your play which limited your excellence, focus your imagination on it and calmly resolve to work harder physically, mentally and tactically — to lift that aspect of your game to the standard that your ability demands. Winning involves a lot of hard work.

Some General Suggestions For All Sports

In its essence, sport involves competition and the eventual dominance of an individual or team over another. No philosophizing or incantations about the joys of playing or the fun associated with playing sport in the right spirit can detract from the simple fact that we all like winning. Think of your attitude to sport now.

We believe that if personal honesty prevails, and that even if you belong to that group who 'play sport to get fit', your conclusion will be that you would much rather win than lose. You do enjoy winning, and you enjoy dominating the opposition. Accept this fact and start mobilizing your thoughts in that direction. Become win-oriented. Say to yourself: 'I enjoy winning. I will lose in the right spirit, gracefully accepting a loss as a measure of my limits. But I will *always* play to win.'

As an aid in this direction it pays to think big, not in terms of ultimate goals (although these are important and will be discussed below) but rather, you should think big about you, yourself, and your abilities. Far too often — and this goes for the Olympic champion right through to the weekend competitor—people underestimate themselves and demean their abilities. They enter the competition arena and see their opposition warming-up and immediately think: 'My God they're good' or 'Good grief they're big' or 'Shit he's strong (fast, powerful, loose, hot. . .' you can go on and on) until they lose themselves in the glorification of their opponent's ability.

Such a glorification represents negative thinking and negative self-suggestion which will eventually be transformed into a hesitant approach to the game and a loss. You don't need to invoke God, grief or excreta to explain away your opponent's abilities. You are in the same class, otherwise you wouldn't be matched in the same contest. Never allow yourself to be overawed by the opposition; remember that when you are warming-up you too will be equally as impressive to an outside observer. Always relish the clash with a good opponent and savour the exquisite challenge of an encounter where you will be tested to your limits. And as a starting point, see no end to your limits. See yourself as bigger, better, stronger, looser. . . hotter. . . than the opposition. See yourself as a big, hard-headed competitor who relishes the testing opportunities and challenges of top competition. This is a suggestion which can be applied at any time during a competition season but for maximum impact and long-term benefit it should be the subject of practice before the competition season commences. Then you are confident and positive, even before you pick up the cudgel.

Now to another general point. Most sports thrive on and glorify that image of our world, the ball. Control the ball and you control the world. All those demands that relate to 'watching the ball', 'get the ball' or 'fight for possession' refer to the pivotal role of the ball in modern sport. In real terms, he who catches, gains, falls on, kicks or hits the ball is in the dominant position. It is the one time when you actually have a say in the course and outcome of a contest — your catching, gaining, falling, kicking or hitting is dictating the next stage in the encounter. And what better subject for a bit of positive self-suggestion?

If you are one of the ninety-odd per cent of sportsmen who compete in a ball-game, then a little self-hypnosis and self-suggestion relating to that ball will not go astray. Centre your imagination on clear images of the ball. See the colour, texture and all the fine detail of the ball of your choice. Focus on that image until it is a clear and decisive picture in your mind. As the focus of your attention, it can be very diverting and relaxing in the same way that concentration on breathing or numbers is a tool in inducing relaxation. Create a clear image of that ball in your mind and then — and this is the crux of the image — see yourself anticipating the movement of the ball and reacting to that movement. Three words: seeing, anticipating and reacting. Those words can be very useful to you in preparing for a contest. A ritual built around seeing the ball is a simple and relevant means of arousing oneself before a contest. Keep this, and the ball, in your mind at all times. It is the basis of most sports and deserves to be the basis of your mental suggestion and preparation for a contest.

Now to the general problem of goals: what are they, how important are they, and how do you achieve them? Very basic questions.

In our outline of a champion's progress, we stressed the importance of goals in the psychological preparation and progression of the champion. For the weekend competitor the goals don't need to be so elaborate as to extend over a full season of competition. A goal is whatever we make it: it can be as simple as getting to training on time through to a general resolution to improve your percentage of wins. Name yourself a goal, map out a pathway to that goal and then don't deviate from it — applying reassurance and reinforcement of that goal at crucial points along the path. More elaboration on goal seeking and achievement is available in the section dealing with the development of a champion.

For the purposes of this general discussion we have divided competitive sport into four categories. These categories, with examples of representative sports, are:

Group contests: swimming and running races
One-to-one contests: tennis, table tennis, fencing
Team contests: football, baseball, basketball
Individual contests: golf, high-jump, weight-lifting

We recognize the difficulties associated with this categorization since the categories overlap. For example, in team sports the clash of attacking and defending players is a clear example of a one-to-one confrontation. However, we will persist with our categorization since there are some unique points in each category which are important in the psychological preparation for competition.

Group Contests

These contests generally emphasize strength, power and endurance and the raw competition of running or swimming harder and faster than the opposition. And here the thrust of self-suggestion should be focused on the body. Always think 'big'—seeing yourself as stronger, more powerful and more enduring than your opposition. Imagine and feel the depth of your breathing and see the huge volume of oxygen coursing through your body energizing all your big, hard-working muscles. See yourself easily busting through pain barriers—because you are tough and strong and determined to win—and the pain means nothing to you because you have goals and you want the reward of achieving that goal. Victory, means more to you than the transient discomfort of oxygen starvation; in fact you revel in the 'high' associated with oxygen starvation. But, and it's a big but, assure yourself that you can tell the difference between a true injury and the passing pain caused by lack of oxygen. And stop when it is an injury.

It is very important in this type of contest to set yourself goals relating to muscular performance and times. Realistic and *attainable* goals. There is no point in setting a goal which is physically impossible in your present state of fitness. Set yourself reasonable goals, increasing through small increments—a determination to cut your time for running 400 metres by five seconds could be broken into ten 'minor' goals of decreases of 0.5 of a second. Concentrate your imagination and energy on the means of achieving your five-second goal—by visualizing the style you need or the simple hard work which is necessary to tune-up your body. And with every successful closing of one of those half-second gaps give yourself a reward—a book, record or dinner—and then get back onto the path of goal seeking.

One-to-one Contests

In these contests the emphasis of the competition situation is confrontation and here, more so than in any other category, it pays to think and be tough, and know that your sporting ability will prevail in the end. The key word, the key suggestion, is willpower since the confrontation situation demands a cool head and the confidence and the ability to stick to a game plan even when all the points seem to be going against you. Learn to alter or adjust the game-plan in tune with developments in play. To be able to *contrive* to win and combine this with the very basic *will* to win is an essential psychological component in the one-to-one contest.

To this end see yourself as a hard-minded, active and strong player who cannot be diverted from the task of winning points. Imagine yourself playing every point on its merits, with the actual score being one of the lowest priorities in your mind. Your priorities should be: first, your level of arousal and the way you are playing; second, how your opponent responds. Your concern over the score should be way down any list. Practise forgetting the score. Concentrate only on playing your best, for each and every point.

But even when you are playing each point as it comes, there will be a time when you play a bad stroke. For many players, one bad stroke serves to cripple them. Wallowing in self-pity and anger over one bad play, they effectively lose the whole contest. One bad play is not that important in the outcome of any contest, so imagine yourself laughing off a bad stroke. See yourself pausing for a moment to consider what happened, imagine yourself playing out the stroke correctly and then actually doing it. In the contest arena follow this formula. Play that bad stroke again and *know* that the next time you are confronted with a similar situation, you will react correctly and spontaneously because you have such a cool head that you are capable of learning from your mistakes.

Another crucial contribution of willpower to the one-to-one contest lies in the emphasis of these contests on speed and co-ordination. It is essential that you have faith in your ability. Any self-doubts will be quickly translated into a loss of speed and co-ordination as you equivocate over your playing ability. Before a contest take time off to see yourself playing at your top. Focus on speed, co-ordination and your winning style.

Team Contests

It is impossible to separate the individual and the team's psychological preparation into neat compartments. It is also impossible to ignore the coach's influence on this preparation. The role of the coach in the physical and psychological preparation of his charges is one of the major factors in a successful season.

We have already discussed some of the important attributes of a good coach. In summary these include: knowledge and authority in the game, ability to command player respect combined with the ability to inspire the individual player and the team as a whole. In his inspirational role the coach should be aiming to develop that nebulous concept of 'team spirit'.

Every coach has his own ideas on the development of this spirit but probably the commonest starting point — in fact so common that it is hardly recognized as such — is the adoption of a team nickname. Often this nickname is chosen as an easy handle for team supporters to grasp; but it should be seen as more than that, since an appropriate nickname combining fighting images and words is a powerful tool in the cultivation of a team spirit.

During both group and individual relaxation sessions, themes associated with the nickname should be developed. Team sessions with the coach or trainer, manipulating words in pursuit of a team theme, is the best approach and it is a wise move to prepare a basic script for these 'team consciousness sessions'. With nicknames such as 'Steelers', 'Cannons', 'Bulldogs' and 'Panthers' it is easy to develop a short story around the virtues and eventual success of the team. The script should be positive but low-key, never touching on past failures, being only concerned with the future which can be built on past glories: 'I want you to remember the time. . . of past victory. . .' Such a script does not need to be of a high literary quality. Remember the team will be in a relaxed and uncritical frame of mind and they will accept and act upon any ideas or suggestions that are proffered. Team sessions should be instituted regularly during the season and can have particularly beneficial effects after either a big win or a bad loss.

For the individual player the emphasis of psychological preparation should be on his role in the team play. Glamorous ideas of 'star' play and selection in a representative side should not be dominant—although selection in a representative side should be aimed at as a long-term goal. But star play or individual play in a team sport is out. You become a 'star' by blending in with the team. The individual with stardom in his mind is often disappointed and disillusioned when team and individual performance do not match up to expectations. You eventually become recognized as a 'star' by doing your job just a little bit better and more consistently than your opposing player.

You achieve star status by concentrating on your team role and the very basics of the game—whether it be running, tackling, batting, ball-handling or catching, or any combination of these skills. Focus your attention and imagination on the basics of the sport and, if you want to be a star, take your cues from our section on programming a champion. Always see yourself playing out your team role efficiently and fluently, with the fact that you are completely dominating your opposition being only incidental to your important role as a team player.

Individual Contests
In this section we have a very diverse collection of sports ranging from high-arousal sports such as weight-lifting and shot-put through to such low-arousal sports as golf and bowling. Although it could be expected that this section would be one of the most difficult in which to generalize, this is not the case. In all sports in the individual category the most basic generalization is that the participant is really only competing against himself—and this has a number of important implications in the psychological preparation.

In these competitions, the player already has some idea of how good he or she is. To win a contest or championship the player knows whether he needs to improve his performance or whether his present level of competence is sufficient to give him victory. The weightlifter who can consistently lift 180 kilos or the golfer who regularly shoots in the low 70s can have reasonable expectations that they will be able to duplicate those efforts in a contest. Knowledge of their opposition coupled with the individual's own desire to win, dictates whether they maintain the steady-state or move to improve themselves. The capacity for establishing and chasing goals is greater in the individual contest than in any of our other categories. If you want to succeed, make use of this capacity for goal setting and self-improvement. As we mentioned earlier, set yourself reasonable and attainable goals which culminate in one broad achievement.

The development of a 'hard-headed' competitor should also be high on the list of the individual performer's priorities. Training yourself to ignore the extraneous influences of crowds and surroundings should be the focus of your imagination. This 'concentration' should be coupled with the fine-tuning of the optimum arousal level, especially since, in these sports, time is not of immediate importance and the competitors have the opportunity to focus on the task at hand and prepare themselves for the performance. Use this time to arouse yourself correctly. Establish a routine and imagine yourself going through this routine — whether it be warming-up by shuffling the feet, short sprints, practice strokes or other exercises. Go through this routine before every performance and, before the start of the contest, lie back and relax yourself and see yourself going through this routine as though you were actually in the contest, and couple these imaginings with positive images of you performing in this contest.

One final generalization about individual contests: there is a great emphasis on style. For this reason a large part of the self-hypnosis and self-suggestion sessions should be focused on this important component of your game — examine and magnify and then correct any faulty body movements See yourself playing in the style you wish to play. See yourself performing with effortless grace with your body movements finely tuned. So much for general, but important hints. We now need to get back to the individual.

You know what you want out of sport, you know the way you like to play and you know the goals you wish to reach. And when we get down to it, it is basically up to *you*. While we have provided ideas and routines which will assist you, it is up to you to apply them.

11
A GUIDE TO SELF-HYPNOSIS

The time has come to outline some techniques for inducing self-hypnosis. Before doing this, there are two points which must be stressed.

First, there is nothing unusual in the use of the term 'self-hypnosis'. The terms 'hypnosis' and 'self-hypnosis' should be considered to be interchangeble: since *all hypnosis is self-hypnosis*. The person who pays a visit to a professional hypnotist in reality hypnotizes himself; the hypnotist is simply a guide or a teacher, a guide who can point out the best way to the relaxed state which is the very basis of hypnotic therapy.

Secondly, there have been many stories written about hypnosis over the years — some true, many false. Most of us have heard something about hypnosis, but most of what you have heard is wrong and misleading. Nearly everyone who is about to be hypnotized for the first time has a preconceived idea of what the trance state is like. It varies from 'like being asleep' to 'like being unconscious' and 'like having an anaesthetic'. It is important for the person about to attempt self-hypnosis to have an insight into the state they are about to enter, since a large percentage of people strive to attain a state that does not exist — a state they imagine to be hypnosis. Be aware of this before attempting self-hypnosis.

Modern hypnotists have now eliminated the word 'sleep' from their induction techniques, and replaced it with 'relaxation' or 'more deeply relaxed'. Mentioning the word 'sleep' indicates to the subject that he or she is in fact going to sleep, but as the induction progresses and they find themselves still awake, they then begin to have doubts about their ability to be hypnotized. They realize that they are still very much awake and aware of other noises and sounds as well as the hypnotist's voice. This creates a barrier and in a lot of cases prevents the successful induction of hypnosis or self-hypnosis. However, when a person being hypnotized or practising self-hypnosis for the first time realizes and understands that hypnosis is only a 'state of super-relaxation', then the whole procedure becomes easier.

You most certainly do not become unconscious and you do not go to sleep. You are fully aware of your surroundings at all times, you know exactly where you are and what you are doing. If anything, the sense of hearing becomes more acute while in the hypnotic state. Hypnosis is nothing more or less than an advanced state of relaxation and the closest we can go to describing it is to get you to imagine your feelings just before you open your eyes after a good night's sleep: you can hear someone in the kitchen rattling the cups. From the sounds you know who's doing it; it's Bob, because of his shuffling feet. You are aware of the morning sounds and everything that's going on around you. You are warm and comfortable but still haven't opened your eyes — in fact you'd like to go back to sleep but the day's reponsibilities are looming. You forget about these responsibilities and snuggle down and enjoy just a few moments more of the comfort and relaxation of your bed until you reluctantly open your eyes and face the day.

In our experience the best way to learn self-hypnosis is to have a session with a professional hypnotist and get him to give you the post-hypnotic suggestion. In the future, you will be able to take yourself back into this state of relaxation by working through a given routine, such as: 'Get comfortable, close your eyes, take three deep breaths and count slowly from one up to ten. By the time you reach the count of ten, you will be in a far more deeply relaxed state than that which you are in now and every time you go into this relaxed state you will become even more deeply relaxed than the time before.'

However, people can hypnotize themselves without any assistance from a professional hypnotist. People have hypnotized themselves by concentrating on the reflective line markers on a lonely night drive along a highway; others can relax and enter a hypnotic state by shutting out the boring drone of an irrelevant lecturer or concert recital, others can do it by listening to the dripping of a tap at night, the clickety-clack of a train going over the joins in the rail or the ticking of a clock or a metronome. *You* can hypnotize yourself by transposing the words in this book onto a tape.

Before we provide specific formulas for self-hypnosis you

should make sure that you are fully aware of the stages in the hypnotic procedure and the importance of that cycle of suggestion and relaxation, followed by further suggestion. You should feel calm and assured about the use and benefits that can be attained through the medium of self-hypnosis. Let us now elaborate on some of the more practical aspects of self-hypnosis.

The Induction Technique

We present two scripts for inducing self-hypnosis. These scripts are best transcribed onto tape and used as a pattern to work to, in order to enter a relaxed state; that state we recognize as hypnosis.

As you will see, the scripts are very simple; that is the essence of the hypnotic procedure. Simple suggestions, simple words suggested again and again, are used to bypass the critical censor present in your conscious, analytical mind. Anything more complex will alert your critical censor and turn your self-hypnosis session into a self-defeating, self-questioning, analytical session. This must be avoided. Do nót question. Concentrate only on what is being said, creating a mental picure in your mind of yourself doing exactly what is being said on the tape. Just flow with the tape, following the instructions exactly.

One thing which could raise the hackles of your critical censor is the simple sound of your own voice. Some people are surprised when they first hear their own voice on tape. So remind yourself what a professional hypnotist will sound like: droning, soothing, relaxing but authoritative. If you still have any doubts about your own voice, then get a friend whose voice has some of the above qualities to read the script into a tape recorder.

It often helps to play a piece of music — definitely not hyperactive rock but a soothing piece from the classics or jazz such as a Brahms Lullaby — behind the recording of the scripts. We leave the choice to you, as you know best what relaxes you.

And, for a further qualification, since every person differs in their quirks and sensibilities and their capacity for absorbing the proffered suggestion, these tapes should not be viewed as the ultimate recipe for self-hypnosis. If a particular word grates on your sensibilities, please change it. Feel free to change the words to suit your own needs, because this is *self*-hypnosis and *you* are allowed to adapt the scripts to suit *your own* needs.

The immediate question that arises here is: 'If I haven't experienced the hypnotic state how do I know what my needs are?

We may sound as if we are escaping our responsibilities, but we can only state that your aims and needs are directed towards achieving a *totally* relaxed state, a relaxed state from which you will arise feeling alert, refreshed, tension-free and inspired by the positive suggestions you have placed in your subconscious mind. You know how to relax. You know when you are feeling alert, with a brain as clear and functional as a bell. This is what you must aim for.

Practice with these tapes until you are satisfied that you can achieve a state of profound relaxation. Then offer yourself the suggestion that we mentioned earlier: 'I will get comfortable, close my eyes, take three deep breaths and count slowly from one to ten. By the time I reach the count of ten I will be in a far more deeply relaxed state than that which I am in now. Far more deeply relaxed than I've ever been before. And every time I practise I will become even more deeply relaxed.' This is a cumulative process that becomes more powerful and more effective each time the tape is played. We cover in more detail the way to use each suggestions in the section below.

Suggestion and the Power of a Mental Image

In both of the scripts presented here, there are gaps to allow you to formulate a suggestion, implanting it in your susceptible, relaxed mind—a mind which is ready to accept and act upon the proffered sugestion.

Leave about a two-minute gap in your tape for your own positive suggestion. You can mentally formulate the suggestion during this period You can say this to yourself, out loud, or you can read your suggestion onto the tape, erasing it once you have successfully acted upon the suggestion, and perhaps replacing it with another more relevant suggestion.

The proffered suggestion must be simple and short but, above all, to the point. Limit your suggestions to one or two at any time. Don't crowd the gap. Remember, the success or failure of self-hypnosis hinges not so much on the depth of relaxation achieved, but on finding and regularly using a compatible suggestion pattern. In Chapter 10 we dealt more specifically with suggestions you may care to use, suggestions which relate to specific sports but can also provide examples of the type of suggestion that you can formulate to suit *your* specific problem, *your* needs.

Mincing words, umming and aahing, with only a vague knowledge of what you want to programme your subconscious mind to do, is not conducive to successful conditioning through self-hypnosis. *The choice of an appropriate suggestion is critical.*

Analyse your performance, your shortcomings and faults. Reread the previous chapter for specific examples of suggestions you could use. Remember, the sub-conscious mind does not analyse, it accepts and acts on *all suggestions* that reach it. You must eliminate any suggestions which come into a neutral or negative category. Positive suggestion is the name of the game.

And, since some people have difficulty in forming mental images or just imagining things, it often helps to write out specific suggestions on a card, which can be glanced at before the hypnotic procedures begin.

If you find that your mind wanders away from the script on occasions, and you become aware of this happening, immediately direct yourself back to concentrating on what is being said. You are relaxing, deeply. You are focusing on one thing: your game.

And when you are in this relaxed state, in addition to giving yourself specific instructions — to correct faulty technique, to overcome fatigue, to be more determined, more aggressive. . . it is a good idea to form mental images of yourself performing at your best. Imagine yourself beating other competitors effortlessly, in international and national competition. See yourself on the winning dais, accepting the winning prize. Do this often. Make your goals high, believe in your ability to reach them. Don't slavishly repeat to yourself, about your tennis game, say, 'serve and volley'. No, imagine yourself serving a hard, perfectly placed, slicing serve which forces your opponent to place the ball exactly where you want it. . . and you use your favourite forehand volley to slip in an easy match-winning point. Visualize yourself playing the best game you've ever played in your life: smashing down aces, moving up to the net quickly and volleying a winner, playing better than you've ever played before.

See yourself in the role or position you wish to be in following a successful course of self-hypnosis, but, and it is an important but, see yourself as *you* wish to be, not as you want other people to see you. Remember, it is *self*-hypnosis, the emphasis is on you not on what other people think about you. Visualize yourself playing the strokes you want to play, running the way you want to run, as if watching your image on film.

The Attitude to the Self-Hypnotist

As you can gather from the above, the attitude of the self-hypnotist is crucial to the successes that may flow from the use of this form of hypnosis. Important aspects of the 'right' attitude are the aims and motives of the practitioner.

Don't delude yourself to the extent that you expect self-hypnosis to produce miracles. You must set realistic goals. The uneducated labourer who suggests to himself 'I will become a brain surgeon' is doomed to fail. However, if his primary suggestion is 'I will return to high school and graduate from high school' with the secondary images of university and medical school in the back of his mind — secondary images only allowed to surface and be emphasized once our friend has completed high school — then he stands a much better chance of becoming a brain surgeon. A realistic goal and attainment of that goal can only spur one on to further successes.

The other side of the coin is the 'right' motive. The person who wants to practise self-hypnosis to remove feelings of guilt about extra-marital adventures is treading on dangerous ground: a fragile psyche; that person needs professional hypnotherapy, not self-hypnosis. With conditions such as this it is vitally important that a form of hypnoanalysis be employed in order to discover the basic cause or repression and facilitate a permanent solution to the problem. This area must be completely avoided by the person using self-hypnosis for motivation and self improvement.

Similarly, individuals who wish to practise self-hypnosis so they can get by on four hours' sleep a night, or athletes who wish to blot out completely any pain felt during the course of a competition, are toying with the possibility of inflicting real harm on their bodies. Their motives are wrong and they risk doing great damage to their physical health since their body will break long before their will; they will not achieve their goals and conclude that their self-hypnosis sessions have all been wasted.

Yes, reasonable motives and realistic goals all contribute to the sum that equals the right attitude, a total formula which will bring you success.

You must have a clear image in your mind of what you hope to achieve, recognizing that you can achieve this through the use of self-hypnosis and feeling relaxed and confident about the use of hypnosis. You must want to attain the hypnotic state and expect to reach it, but above all you must let yourself go into the hypnotic state. The keywords here are: *want* it, *expect* it, and then *let* it. Want it to happen, expect it to happen and then let it happen.

Setting

The setting is especially important in the first sessions of self-hypnosis. The ideal physical setting is a warm room (around 23-25°C) free from draughts with a low light level and very, very quiet. It is important that you are warm and comfortable since it is known that under cold conditions it is very difficult to induce hypnosis. Under extremely cold conditions, where the critical censor is very active, it is virtually impossible to hypnotize oneself because, while you are telling yourself to relax, your critical censor knows you are cold and uncomfortable and it is impossible to relax with muscles shivering to warm you.

Your aim should be to reduce or eliminate any noise, sights or other sensory inputs which may alert your critical censor and distract you from the induction procedure. A great aid in achieving such conditions is the use of headphones to listen to the taped induction method. Excess noise is, after cold, probably the greatest distraction you will encounter in your efforts to hypnotize yourself.

Ideally, and with the induction formula on tape, you should place yourelf in a warm, dark, soundproof room. Lie on a bed or sit in a comfortable chair, lean back, get comfortable, put your headphones on and switch on the tape recorder.

Unfortunately these sort of conditions are difficult to obtain in our noisy lives. Kids squawking, radios playing, phones ringing, people shuffling around outside the door, traffic . . . all contribute to the constant intrusions into our private inner space.

If you want to enter your private inner space, you must find a quiet niche in which to practise. There are places that you can adapt to your purposes. If you have a private office, take the phone off the hook, put up a 'do not disturb' sign, place your feet up on the desk, lean back and relax — listening to your tape. And if noises intrude, such as the chatter of a typewriter, use those noises: turn them into an induction aid by suggesting to yourself that with every line you can hear being typed, you are relaxing more, going deeper and deeper into the relaxed state you are trying to achieve.

Self-hypnosis can even be practised during a daily train trip. The rolling, clattering rhythm of a train can be conducive to entering the hypnotic state, especially when there are long gaps between stations. In this case find a seat and, using a portable cassette recorder, lean back and relax.

Again we emphasize that, if you want to attain the hypnotic state, you will find a time and place to practise.

With ample practice you will find that you don't need the tape and the setting is unimportant. You will find that you are using your own technique — three deep breaths and a count to ten, followed by relaxation coursing through your body, perhaps combined with an appropriate suggestion — to induce hypnosis whenever you want to: before an important meeting, between greens in a game of golf, after a tense and tiring day, between sets in a hard and crucial game of tennis, at half time in a football game, or in the hour preceding competition.

Success and Failure

Like so many other human activities, success with self-hypnosis comes only through constant practice. There is no point in starting if you think that one session with the taped induction will bring you instant results. One session will not convert a B-grade loser into an A-grade winner. But integration of self-hypnosis into the general training and practice routine of your chosen sport may provide a successful formula.

Remember at all times that your tape recording is simply a pattern to work to. You must work at it. The harder you work at it, the more time you put into it — we recommend that you listen to the tape at least once a day, preferably twice a day. The more you practise forming the mental image of doing exactly what your tape suggests, the sooner you will achieve your aims.

As we mentioned earlier, a problem that occurs with people who are learning self-hypnosis from scratch is that they do not know what they are looking for in the hypnotic state — they want reassurance that they have relaxed and that they have entered a hypnotic trance. Such reassurance can only come through a visit to a professional hypnotist, but it is worth remembering that the depth of trance is not so crucial for the success of self-hypnosis. It has been generally recognized that the success or failure of hypnosis is not due to the depths of relaxation achieved, but to finding and regularly using the right suggestion pattern.

Another problem that often arises in self-hypnosis is that people *try too hard*. And, because they are striving so hard to achieve the hypnotic state, they tense up; a situation which is incompatible with hypnosis. If you find this occurring, immediately concentrate on relaxing. Two or three deep breaths will help deflect you back to concentrating on what is being said on the tape. You cannot force your mind to accept your suggestions but you can wheedle them in, once your mind is totally relaxed. Remember, you must adopt a detached attitude; *wanting* the hypnotic state, *expecting* it, and then *letting* it occur.

One final problem that often arises is that when people try to practise self-hypnosis in their own homes, they are afraid to let themselves go — they wish to maintain some contact with the outside world. In a hypnotist's office, such people have the security of the droning presence of the hypnotist's voice plus the reassurance that no one is going to intrude into the privacy of that office. At home the individual, in many cases, has an instinctive need to hang on to reality — through a fear that the house will burn down, the doorbell will ring or there will be a telephone call.

This fear of *letting go* may be overcome by a visit to the privacy of a hypnotist's office, where you can really let yourself go, or by offering yourself the suggestion that you will relax, relax deeply and, if the doorbell rings. . . you will open your eyes, arise, and feel totally refreshed, totally alert and capable of handling any situation. At any time, if you wish to awaken from the hypnotic state, all you have to do is say 'I will wake up on the count of three — one, two, three'. And you will be wide awake and back to normal.

The Script

Pause briefly after every paragraph.

Where a paragraph is marked * this means that you should have a slightly longer pause *before* reading it.

At the section marked 'GAP', leave a two minute pause on the tape where you can record the suggestions you wish to act upon. You can erase these when you wish, recording fresh ones, or you can leave the two-minute gap blank and just enjoy the pleasure of relaxation.

Script 1

On this tape you are going to learn how to relax and, as a means to this end, I want you to follow my every word.

I also want you to let your mind flow. Let your mind wander with my words. I want you to imagine the meanings behind my words. To imagine the feelings behind my words.

*First of all I want you to imagine yourself out walking on a fine, warm sunny day and you come to a large, inviting tunnel, set between two lovely hills.

Imagine you are at the edge of the tunnel, just standing there, looking down into the tunnel. The tunnel is sloping slightly downwards, is dimly lit, but very inviting. Your curiosity is aroused so you begin walking down into the tunnel, one foot in front of the other.

It is pleasantly warm in the dim light, just walking down, down, down into the tunnel. You can hear footsteps echoing way down the tunnel in front of you.

And, way in the distance you can see a little chink of light, so you begin walking towards it.

And, as you get closer to that distant chink of light, you realize that it's coming from underneath a doorway, so you walk right up to the doorway, you open the door and you step right into the room.

*You have a look around and you can see yourself lying on a bed, so you close the door behind you, and you walk across the room, and you're now standing up beside the bed, looking down at yourself.

*Notice how relaxed you are.

Notice how slow and even your breathing is. Notice how your pulse rate has slowed down considerably — you can tell this by looking at the little artery at the side of your neck.

And now you turn around and you sit down on top of yourself. You swing your legs up and around and you lie right back, melting into your own body.

Just melting into your own body.

And as you do this you relax more and more deeply.

Deep, deep relaxation.

And now I want you to take three deep breaths, right in as far as you can, and right out as far as you can. Just allowing yourself to relax more and more deeply. Deep, deep relaxation.

*Now, as I name the parts of the body I want you to make a special effort to relax them just a little bit more.

Starting off with your feet, just let your feet relax. The muscles in your instep, your ankles — just let them relax right-off, completely.

The calf muscles at the back of your legs — just let them relax also.

Up the front of your shins, the muscles in your thighs — let them become heavy, limp, loose and relaxed.

Your stomach muscles. First of all I want you to tense them a little, tighten them up.

*And now let them relax right-off, completely. Completely.

On the count of three I want you to take a very deep breath, right in as far as you can, then right out as far as you can. And, as you release that breath, all the muscles in your chest will relax right-off, completely.

One.

Two.

Three.

Deep breath, right in as far as you can.

And now right out as far as you can.

*Just allowing yourself to relax right-off, completely.

Shrug your shoulders a little bit.

Allow all of the muscles in your shoulders to relax, right-off, completely.

And now allow that relaxation to creep down your shoulders, over the ends, down your arms, past your elbows and right on to the very tips of your fingers. Allow your fingers to relax, right-off, completely.

*Loose, limp, heavy, and completely relaxed.

The muscles in your forehead, just let them relax also. Your eyelids, especially your eyelids, just imagine that they are made of lead and they're drooping down, very, very tightly. Loose, limp, heavy.

Heavy and relaxed.

The facial muscles, the muscles around your jaw and chin, let them become loose, limp, heavy and very relaxed.

Now I want you to concentrate very hard on what I'm going to say next. I want you to imagine, I want you to really imagine, that you're actually doing everything I'm talking about.

I want you to imagine, as I count slowly from one to three, that your eyelids themselves are sticking together, very, very tightly.

*One, just imagine that your eyelids are sticking together very, very tightly.

Two, imagine that they're sticking together, tighter and tighter, as if there were glue and cement between your eyelids, sticking them down, gripping them down, tighter and tighter still.

Three, they're so tightly stuck together now that you can't open them. You can try but its impossible. You cannot open your eyes. But don't try any more. Just take another deep breath, right in as far as you can, relaxing more and more.

*You are now in a position where you can give yourself any positive suggestions that you wish to give. Any suggestions given at this time will have a positive effect upon you.

(GAP)

You are going to be affected by all the positive suggestions on this tape. You want to be affected, you know you will and you can expect to be affected.

I'm going to wake you up now. On the count of three you are going to awake, feeling fresh and relaxed, mentally alert and completely tension free, remembering all of the things, the good important things that you have just told yourself, knowing them and believing them to be true.

One. Waking slowly, but you can't open your eyes yet.

Two. Nearly awake.

Three. Wide awake, wide awake. Wake up now.

Script 2

On this tape you are going to learn how to relax and, as a means to this end, I want you to follow my every word.

I also want you to let your mind flow. Let your mind wander with my words. I want you to imagine the meanings behind my words. To imagine the feelings behind my words.

First of all I want you to clench your right fist. Very tightly, tighter still, just like an oyster shell closing.

*Here we have a typical example of tension. Look at your fist. See how tensed it is. Feel how tensed it is.

And now relax your hand and allow your fingers to hang down limply.

See how relaxed it is. See how it is exactly the opposite of the way it was before. You now realize that it is not possible to be tense and relaxed at the same time. Because they are opposites.

Now I want you to get as comfortable as possible. Either by sitting up or lying down.

Close your eyes.

Just allow your eyes to close. It's easier to concentrate with your eyes closed.

Take a deep breath in as far as you can. Allowing your whole body to relax as much as possible.

*Now as I name the parts of the body, I want you to make a very special effort to relax them as much as possible.

Starting off with your feet. Just allow them to become very heavy, limp, relaxed. All of the muscles around your toes, your instep, your ankle, just allow them to relax and become as heavy as lead.

The calf muscles at the back of your legs. Allow them to become heavy and relaxed. Loose, heavy and relaxed.

Up the front of your shins. Allow that heaviness to creep up the front of your shins. Allow them to become limp, heavy and relaxed.

The muscles in your thighs. Just allow them to relax. And the front of your thighs, and up the back of your thighs. You feel that there is a peaceful, heavy, lazy feeling creeping over your whole body. You feel very comfortable and pleasantly relaxed. You have the feeling that you couldn't care less about anything.

And every breath you take relaxes you more and more.

*Now the muscles in your stomach. First of all I want you to tense them.

Make them hard.

Now let them relax-off, completely. Let them become loose,

heavy, limp and relaxed. All tension is leaving your body. And now you can feel a warm glowing feeling in your stomach and it's beginning to spread right down your legs and right up into your chest.

And now, on the count of three, I want you to take a very deep breath, right in as far as you can and right out as far as you can.

And as you release that breath, all tension will go right out of your chest. The whole of your chest will become heavy, limp and relaxed.

One.

Two.

Three.

Deep breath right in.

And now right out as far as you can. Just allowing all the muscles in your chest to relax right-off, completely. Completely.

And now allow that relaxation to go into your shoulders. Shrug your shoulders a little bit.

Now allow them to relax, let them become very heavy, loose, limp and completely relaxed.

Allow that relaxation to run right down your arms, past your elbows, down to the tips of your fingers.

Now wriggle your fingers, and allow them to relax even more.

Your neck. Just allow the muscles at the front of your neck to relax. Allow them to become loose also.

Allow that relaxation to creep down over your shoulder blades and then right down the rest of your back. Allowing your whole body to become heavy, heavier still, limp and completely relaxed.

Your eyebrows. Just raise your eyebrows a little.

And now allow them to come down again, relaxing the muscles in your forehead and your eyelids.

Especially your eyelids, they feel as though big weights have been attached to the bottom of them and are dragging them down, heavy, loose, limp and completely relaxed.

You have the feeling that you just couldn't care less about anything.

Such a wonderful feeling. You have never felt so relaxed, for such a long, long time, as you do at this very moment.

Now I want you to concentrate very hard on what I'm going to say next.

I want you to imagine you are actually doing what I'm talking about. I want you to imagine that you are on holiday and you have gone for a stroll along a deserted beach.

You spread out your towel, you lie down and relax completely.

Its such a peaceful place. Completely quiet except for the sound of the wind and waves and the occasional call of a seagull.

The sun is pleasantly warm, you feel drowsy, limp, all your muscles are loose and heavy. All of your tensions are being completely released as you lie there. All of your worries, anxieties, stresses and strains, are being completely released.

They are draining out of your body just like little drops of water dripping off your body and being absorbed into the towel you are are lying on.

It is such a wonderful feeling.

*After a while you realize that the sun is getting hotter but you feel so lazy and relaxed that you can't be bothered moving, yet you realize that if you continue to lie out in the sun you may get too hot and uncomfortable and this is something that you do not want to happen.

So with a big sigh you drag yourself up to your feet and begin walking towards a clump of shady trees a little further along the beach.

When you get there you find a hammock stretched out between two trees, so you climb into it.

And begin to rock gently, backwards and forwards, backwards and forwards, backwards and forwards, backwards and forwards. Such a lovely feeling.

*As you breath in, silently repeat the word 'sleep', as you breath out, silently repeat the word 'deep sleep'.

*Sleep.

*Deep sleep.

After a while you look up through the branches of the trees and notice the clouds going overhead. Big billowy white clouds drifting by, little clouds just floating past. And as you notice this you become lazier and heavier still, more and more relaxed.

Every word I say to you relaxes you more deeply.

Every breath you breathe relaxes you further still.

And now you notice that one of the clouds has detached itself from the others and is gradually coming down to where you are lying on your hammock.

It gradually nestles under your hammock.

Now a gentle breeze comes along, lifting you, the hammock and the cloud right up into the air. You can feel yourself gradually floating, higher and higher.

You are very comfortable, just lying back, bobbing along.

You can now see other clouds all around you. Such a wonderful feeling, just floating along, leaving all of your worries, tensions, anxieties, stresses and strains, far behind you.

As you float along you go deeper and deeper into this wonderful relaxed state.

Now the cloud begins to come down to earth.

Ever so gently, and it is going to land in the most peaceful place you know. Perhaps it is a beach somewhere, or maybe in the mountains or some other place you know.

And now the cloud is landing in this wonderful place. The most comfortable place, the most peaceful place you know.

Serene. Peaceful. The most peaceful place you know.

You are now in the most peaceful place you know.

Such a wonderful place. So relaxing. There is a wonderful feeling of serenity surrounding the whole place. The atmosphere is so different and so unusual. So peaceful.

You are more relaxed than you have ever been at any time in your life.

Now I want you to imagine the following colours. I want you to imagine that you can actually see them.

Perhaps the easiest way to do this is to imagine you see something that is familiar to you and is of the colour that I mention.

*Now just imagine you can see the colour red.

Just the colour red.

And now the colour orange.

*Just seeing the colour orange.

The colour yellow. You can actually see the colour yellow.

*And now the colour green.

Just seeing the colour green.

And now blue. Just seeing the colour blue.

*And now the colour deep purple.

And finally the colour violet. Just seeing the colour violet.

*And now that you have imagined seeing all these colours, you are now more deeply relaxed than you were before.

More relaxed. More comfortable. Such a wonderful feeling.

*And now I'm going to be silent for a few minutes and let you give yourself any positive suggestions that you wish to receive. And, when I begin speaking to you again, the sound of my voice will make you even more deeply relaxed.

(GAP)

Every night while you are asleep, from now on, you will sleep very deeply and very soundly. Awakening only in the event of danger to yourself or any member of your family or household. Everything going all right, you will sleep right through the night until the time you wish to awaken.

You will awake feeling relaxed, refreshed and completely tension free. Looking forward to the day ahead.

Every day from now on, you will get more and more confidence in yourself and everything you do. More confidence in your ability to achieve goals, more confidence in yourself to make decisions, more confidence in your social life. In fact, generally every day you will become more confident in yourself.

And every time you play this tape you will be able to relax more deeply than the time before, far more deeply than you are now.

*I'm going to wake you up now.

On the count of three you will wake up feeling refreshed, relaxed, mentally alert and completely tension-free; remembering the things that have been told to you, believing them and knowing them to be true.

One. Waking slowly.

Two. Nearly awake now.

Three. Completely awake. Wide awake. Wake up.

This completes our discourse on the use of self-hypnosis in sport. We hope that we have filled a big gap in the appreciation of modern sport, but more importantly, we hope the individual will have a greater appreciation of the role of psychology in their favourite sport and be aware that if they have goals, whether it be to a world championship or the simple ⊙ achievement of a happy level of competence, then self-hypnosis can hasten the achievement of those goals. For the individual who aims high, who wants to be 'best', we can only emphasize once more that it's going to be a hard slog. But with a constant concern for your goal and the unified development of the trio of skills that comprise sporting excellence, you can achieve your aim.

Further Reading

The following books provide a broad overview of the theories, techniques and applications of hypnosis:

Barber, T. X., Spanos, N. P., and Chaves, J. F., *Hypnosis, Imagination and Human Potentialities*. Pergamon Press, New York 1974.

Hall, T. and Grant, G., *Superpsych: The Power of Hypnosis*. Methuen Australia, Sydney 1976.

Kroger, W. S., *Clinical and Experimental Hypnosis*. J. B. Lippincott, Philadelphia 1977.

For those interested in various aspects of the psychology of sport, A. Craig Fisher has collected a range of scientific studies which make interesting, if at times difficult, reading:

Fisher, A. Craig, *Psychology of Sport: Issues and Insights*. Mayfield, USA 1976.

A self-improvement series of tapes is available from:

Dr L. Cunningham,
2 Gozo Road,
Greystones, NSW, 2145.
Phone (02) 688 1103.
Motivation Tapes
Learn to Relax, Release Nervous Tension and Live Longer
How to Break the Smoking Habit
Diet Effectively and Easily
Motivate Yourself for Self-Improvement
Develop a Positive Mental Attitude
Self-Hypnosis
How to Improve Your Sporting Performances

Index

New! HYPNOTISM AND MYSTICISM OF INDIA

By Ormond McGill
Dean of American Hypnotists;
author of *"Professional Stage Hypnotism."*

Now you can learn *ORIENTAL HYPNOTISM* as performed by the Masters of India; there are their secret teachings. Noted author and hypnotist Ormond McGill reveals how the real mysticism and magic of India is accomplished. You are taught how to be adept.

The original draft of this book was written in Calcutta in collaboration with the great Hindu Sage, Sadhu Parimal Bandu . . . it may well be called the "textbook" of the Hindu Hypnotists and Magicians, and reveals secrets that have been closely guarded for centuries and known only to the limited view. Now **these secrets can be yours.** Note the remarkable Table of Contents of subjects covered in depth so you can now perform the mysticism and magic of India:

Hindu Fakir Magic, Genuine East Indian Magic, The Science of Pranayama, Oriental Rhythmic Breathing Techniques, Yogi Pranayama Practices, The Mastery of the Mind, The Power of Concentration, Oriental Vizualization and Projection, The Magic Power of Words and Sound, Learning the Art of Maya, Occidental/Oriental Hypnotism, Silent Psychic Influence, Yogi Mental Broadcasting, The Psychic Control of Events, The Magic of Love, The Secrets of Yoga Cosmology, Becoming a Master Magician and Hypnotist, Yama, Yogi Self-Development, The Great "I AM," Index.

You are instructed exactly as the Hindu magicians and hypnotists themselves are instructed, showing you exactly how to develop these remarkable powers. Included are detailed instructions in Oriental Hypnotism which is the finest method of hypnotizing ever developed—combining both Oriental and Occidental techniques. You are shown the Yogi Art of Maya for hypnotically controlling the minds of others. How to Read the Akashic Records, Astral Projection, Yoga Cosmology, and how to perform Yama, the Yoga Method of Self-Hypnosis that can make a man over completely anew.

**Limited First Edition – deluxe and hardbound,
with dust jacket – 208 pages – fully illustrated – $11.50**

Best Seller!
SELF HYPNOSIS
And Other
Mind Expanding Techniques

BROUGHT TOGETHER FOR THE FIRST TIME:
Techniques and How-to of Self-hypnosis,
Auto-suggestion, Behavior Modification,
Faith Healing and Subconscious Reprogramming

By Charles Tebbetts

Much of the material in this book, theoretical as well as practical, was stimulated by the remarkable teachings and influence of an extraordinary man, Gil Boyne, a certified Hypnotherapist who has a Hypnotism Institute just off the campus of U.C.L.A.

I began my studies with Gil Boyne in 1970 and I was quickly captivated by his charisma and personal power. I always had the sense of watching a gifted artist at work when I watched him induce a hypnotic trance in a matter of seconds. I have never seen anyone induce hypnosis as fast as Gil Boyne does. By the end of the course I could hypnotize myself and program my deeper mind in minutes.

Mr. Boyne calls his method of overcoming the negative scripts of the past, "POWER PROGRAMMING"! He has revised the stereotyped concepts of Auto-suggestion and created the first totally new methods in more than forty years!

Gil Boyne teaches his methods to capacity classes five nights a week, and in the many classes I attended I met an extraordinary cross-section of humanity, ranging from aspiring performers to celebrated super-stars and athletes, from bank tellers to corporation presidents. Some of the people I met at Gil Boyne's Self-Help Institute are: commedienne Lily Tomlin; National Bowling Champion Barry Asher; Sylvester Stallone, writer and star of the film "Rocky"; the charismatic TV minister Reverend Ike; Lloyd Haines, TV star of "Room 222"; Lisa Todd of TV's "Hee Haw"; film and TV star Sheree North; famed concert violinist Endre Balogh; writer Jane Wagner (writer-producer for Lily Tomlin). In short, all kinds of people from all walks of life come to study with the man whose methods I described in this book.

Third Edition — 128 pages — softbound — $3.95

Best Seller!
TOTAL MIND POWER

How To Use the Other 90%
of Your Mind

By Donald L. Wilson, M.D.

Now you can unlock the secrets to better health and happiness. Dr. Wilson's revolutionary book shows you the easily learned, but powerful techniques of **Total Mind Power** for tapping the other 90% of your mind.

Benefits of Total Mind Power while you sleep and dream
Increasing memory with Total Mind Power
Stop pain with Total Mind Power
Total Mind Power for better health
Improving eyesight with Total Mind Power
Slowing down the aging process
Increasing sexual responsiveness
Increasing your extrasensory perception
Expanding your religious experiences
Stopping fears and phobias
Changing your weight with Total Mind Power
Stop smoking with Total Mind Power
Improving sports performance
Controlling a tumor with Total Mind Power
Overcoming alcohol and drugs
Using Total Mind Power for emotional stability
General benefits of using Total Mind Power
Motivating yourself to success
Lowering high blood pressure

An extraordinary book, written by a physician who recognizes and uses the patient's power of mind. Explicit and detailed programming suggestions and a comprehensive bibliography make this book a must for all serious students and practitioners of hypnosis!

Illustrated — 256 pages — hardbound — $9.95

You Can Activate the Power of Your Subconscious Mind and...
COME ALIVE!
with SELF HYPNOSIS and "POWER PROGRAMMING"
by Gil Boyne
Authority on Hypnosis Motivation and Mental Programming

CASSETTE TAPE #101 — SELF-CONFIDENCE THROUGH SELF-IMAGE PROGRAMMING
Radiate dynamic self-confidence — Improve your self-image — Overcome the fear of criticism, fear of rejection, fear of failure — Feel more lovable and appreciate yourself more **$9.95**

CASSETTE TAPE #102 — CONCENTRATION — MEMORY — RETENTION — PERFECT RECALL
This method is the only scientifically-validated memory system known — requires no memorization of key words or word associations — liberate your photographic memory — a fool-proof cure for forgetfulness — use your automatic mind search and memory-scanning capacity. The unique methods are placed indelibly into your subconscious mind for your permanent use. **$9.95**

CASSETTE TAPE #103 — DEEP RELAXATION AND RESTFUL SLUMBER
Here is a new way to go to sleep! This incredibly effective and totally safe techpique enables you to shed the cares of the day and drift off within minutes after your head hits the pillow. Your float into a sleep as refreshing and rejuvenating as it is deep. You feel new vitality and energy each morning, and you maintain high energy levels through the day. **$9.95**

CASSETTE TAPE #104 — SECRETS OF SUCCESS ATTITUDES
Overcomes your subconscious "will to fail" — you can learn to move rapidly toward your career and financial goals — success and riches spring from a foundation of "subconscious mental expectancy" — money does not come from high IQ, education, hard work or goodness — begin now to realize the enduring success and wealth that is potentially yours! **$9.95**

CASSETTE TAPE #105 — TRIM AND FIT — VITAL AND HEALTHY
The mental factors in compulsive overeating are widely recognized. This new method conditions your nervous system and your subconscious mind to rapidly move you toward your goal of attractive fitness. Gives you a new self-image about your physical self. Changes your eating habits by changing your appetite desires. Improves your figure easily and quickly. **$9.95**

CASSETTE TAPE #106 — SECRETS OF COMMUNICATION AND EXPRESSION
How to present your ideas in a way that insures acceptance. If you are the one who feels fear and tension at the thought of having to give a speech or a short report, this tape is a blessing! You can speak with absolute confidence and perfect poise, whether to an audience of hundreds or a small group or a single person. **$9.95**

CASSETTE TAPE #107 — DYNAMICS OF CREATIVE ACTING
Program your mind for success in your acting career. Covers auditions, rehearsing, performing, mental attitude and self-image. Overcome, "The Freeze," learn lines quickly and easily. Express your creativity. **$9.95**

CASSETTE TAPE #108 — DYNAMICS OF SELF-DISCOVERY
Answers the question, "WHO AM I?"! Overcomes the identity crisis. Creates a powerful belief in your own abilities. Discover the real self and your true capacity for joyful living! Teaches you how to give yourself — love, acceptance and approval. **$9.95**

CASSETTE TAPE #109 — DYNAMIC HEALTH AND RADIANT VITALITY
You can overcome fears and negative beliefs and your state of health. This program subconsciously develops the mental imagery, feeling tone, and mental expectancy for radiant, vibrant expression of perfect health.

CASSETTE TAPE #112 — DYNAMICS OF CREATIVE WRITING
The hypnotic programming tape that was developed for a producer-writer of a famous dramatic-comedy T.V. show. This writer later claimed that this programming was an important factor in the creation of a script that won an Emmy nomination. **$9.95**

NEW **CASSETTE TAPE #114 — YOU CAN STOP SMOKING NOW!**
This power-programmed cassette will overcome the helpless feeling that underlies tobacco addiction. In just a short time, you become free of tobacco -- permanently! Enjoy a longer, healthier, happier life. **$9.95**

NEW **CASSETTE TAPE #115 — SEXUAL ENRICHMENT FOR MEN**
You have the right to sexual happiness! Powerful desire, total function, and glowing fulfillment is the result of your use of this program. **$9.95**

NEW **CASSETTE TAPE #116 — SEXUAL ENRICHMENT FOR WOMEN**
See description above for #115. **$9.95**

SPECIAL OFFER!

The Gil Boyne Hypnomotivation Series
Any 3 Cassettes — $25.00
Any 6 Cassettes — $45.00

EASY ORDER FORM

FILL IN AND MAIL
...TODAY!

WESTWOOD PUBLISHING CO.

QUANTITY	ITEM NUMBER	DESCRIPTION	UNIT PRICE	TOTAL

POSTAGE & HANDLING
up to $25 add $1.50
$26 to $60 add $2.75
$61 and above add $3.50

TOTAL AMOUNT ALL ITEMS	
POSTAGE AND HANDLING	
6% SALES TAX—CALIF. ONLY	
GRAND TOTAL	

PRINT CLEARLY

COMPANY

NAME

ADDRESS   APT #

CITY   STATE   ZIP

PHONE (AREA CODE)

SIGNATURE X

Note: Your order cannot be processed without a signature

CHARGE MY:
☐ BankAmericard/ Visa
☐ Mastercharge

BANKAMERICARD

master charge

Minimum credit card charge $20.

*Above postage and handling schedule applies to check and credit card orders in Continental U.S. only

Credit Card No

Mastercharge Inter Bank No
(above your name)

Expiration date | Mo | Yr
required

Make check payable to.

GIL BOYNE
312 Riverdale Dr.
Glendale, CA 91204

CALL ORDER DESK AT (213) 242-3497

USE YOUR CREDIT CARD...CHARGE BY PHONE